STYLE

and

SPICE

STYLE

and

SPICE

Over 200 Recipes from the American Southwest

CHEF LARRY EDWARDS

Skyhorse Publishing

STYLE AND SPICE

Skyhorse Publishing books may be purchased in bulk at special discounts for sales promotion, corporate gifts, fund-raising, or educational purposes. Special editions can also be created to specifications. For details, contact the Special Sales Department, Skyhorse Publishing, 307 West 36th Street, 11th Floor, New York, NY 10018 or info@skyhorsepublishing.com.

Skyhorse® and Skyhorse Publishing® are registered trademarks of Skyhorse Publishing, Inc.®, a Delaware corporation.

Visit our website at www.skyhorsepublishing.com.

10 9 8 7 6 5 4 3 2 1

Library of Congress Cataloging-in-Publication Data is available on file.

Cover design by Jane Sheppard
Cover photography by iStock
Interior photography by Casa de Cuisine

Print ISBN: 978-1-5107-2104-3
eBook ISBN: 978-1-5107-2105-0

Printed in China

Table of Contents

Introduction

You are about to embark on what very well may be the most delicious journey of your life. A journey which will take your mouth to every known element of savory and sweet. A journey replete with the natural flavors of nature and the beauty they possess. A journey which will share the subtle heat and the spiritual coolness of one of the most beautiful places on Earth, the great American Southwest. Welcome to *Style and Spice: Over 200 Recipes from the American Southwest*!

In today's health-conscious world, people are not just looking for outstanding flavors, they are looking for nutrition as well; they are looking for natural ingredients; they want to bring "organic" to their dinner tables. There is no other cuisine which implements what people truly want more than the food of the Southwest. Once one has experienced the tastes and textures of true Southwest cuisine, one truly has experienced the full spectrum of Mother Nature's bounty.

As you go through this book, you will find something rather odd when it comes to cookbooks. You will find no use of processed ingredients. True Southwest cuisine is fresh and natural, and this is just one of the reasons why it is considered one of the healthiest cuisines on this planet. Matter of fact, if you research the most popular ingredients of Southwest cuisine (including the various spices), you will even learn that many of them are currently being studied as natural fighters of such diseases as cancer and Alzheimer's. Yes, healthy food can be downright delicious!

While we're on the subject of processed food, you will notice a very special section of this book called The Southwest Pantry. In this section of the book, I will share with you some very simple recipes for items which are often used in the Southwest kitchen and some probably used in your everyday cooking, yet often these are store-bought items loaded with chemicals and preservatives. I will show you how to make them fresh, and not only will the freshness greatly enhance the dishes you are making but, in the long run, it will save you a considerable amount of money.

The Southwest Pantry will go into various glazes, marinades, relishes, and a wonderful selection of the most popular salsas. I'll even tell you how to make tortilla chips, and those rather expensive store-bought flavored oils. Whether you are planning a wonderful Southwest dinner—or any dinner really—I think you will find this section of *Style and Spice: Over 200 Recipes from the American Southwest* to be one which will be useful time and time again.

When we head into **The Southwest Kitchen** and start cooking, I think you will be amazed at the simple elegance of the dishes we have included. From some downright delicious meat dishes, including a bevy of ribs (yeah, we do like our ribs here in the Southwest), a wonderful selection of our Southwest chicken dishes (including our famed Barbecue Fried Chicken), and an assortment of seafood specialties that will literally have your mouth watering. We don't stop with the usual roster most cookbooks have, as out here in the Southwest we also take a great deal of pride in our wonderfully original salads and some of the most refreshing side dishes your dinner table will ever see, all of which go wonderfully with any of the meat, chicken, or seafood entrées included in this book.

Of course, no cookbook on the Southwest would be complete if I didn't share some of our famous cornbreads and delicious desserts. In the section cleverly entitled **The Southwest Oven**, you will get not only the aforementioned cornbreads but some of our most beloved savory breads. When it comes to the breads of the Southwest, we're not too fond of them being boring. Any great meal in the Southwest ends on a sweet note, so of course we include a generous sampling of our desserts. Here in the Southwest, we take our desserts rather seriously. We don't play around with fancy pastries and the like. Who has that kind of time? We rely on nature and goodness, so you'll notice a lot of fresh fruits and, to be honest, some of the best damn frozen desserts your mouth will ever caress, including the original Applewood-Smoked Bacon Ice Cream.

It is my opinion that you really can't enjoy the flavors of the Southwest with a dry mouth and it is for this reason we even have a very special section called **The Southwest Cantina**. Now, if you have ever visited one of the famous cantinas of the Southwest, you are very well aware of the fact that we know how to make a drink! In this section, I will share with you the most popular drinks, from fancy to rugged. If you happen to be a fan of rum or tequila (the two most popular liquors used in our drinks), you will find The Southwest Cantina to perfectly wet your whistle. And of course, we couldn't do a section like this without sharing our recipe for one of the most famous adult beverages in the Southwest: Sangria!

So, now that I have rambled about the food and drink of the great American Southwest, it's time to do some cooking. Fear not, we have made all these dishes extremely easy to prepare, and you won't have to be Marco Polo to find any of the ingredients. They are all available at your local supermarket or the Latino market in your area. You won't find any fancy culinary words used here where you'll have to get out the Ouija board and summon the spirit of Julia Child. It's all about delicious food and flavorful fun—the elements of the true Southwest kitchen.

The Southwest Pantry

Chips

Southwest Chili Chips	5
Casa Tortilla Chips	6
Spicy Plantain Chips	7

Glazes

Whiskey and Maple Glaze	8
Coffee Barbecue Glaze	9
Roasted Garlic Barbecue Glaze	10
Spicy Chipotle Glaze	12
Sherry and Shallot Apple Cider Glaze	14

Ketchups, Mustards, and Mayonnaises

Chili Rojo Mustard	15
Chipotle Mayonnaise	16
Southwest Style Crème Fraîche	17
Cinnamon Scented Ketchup	18
Maple Dill Mustard	19
Gringo Mayonnaise	20
Smoked Chili Ketchup	21
Serrano Chili Mayonnaise	22

Marinades

Gin and Juniper Berry Marinade	23
Citrus Basil Marinade	24
Spicy Lime and Cilantro Marinade	25
Sweet Pepper and Cilantro Marinade	26
Tangerine and Tequila Marinade	27

Oils

Basil Oil	28
Chili Oil	29
Cinnamon Oil	30
Cumin Oil	31
Lemon Oil	32

Relishes

Santa Fe Ginger Relish	33
Five Onion Relish	34
Mint Breeze Mango Relish	35
Bourbon Peach Relish	36

Dry Rubs

Ancho Chili Butter Rub	37
Cumin and Black Pepper Rub	38
Picante Chili Rub	39

Salsas

Red Chili Salsa	40
Citrus Tequila Salsa	41
Green Chili Salsa	42
Hotter Than Hell Salsa	43
Mango Jicama Salsa	44
Multi-Melon Salsa	45
Pineapple Salsa	46
Salsa Fresca	47
Sweet Pepper Salsa	48
Tequila Salsa	49
Tomatillo and Serrano Salsa	50
Salsa Tropical	51

Sauces

Cherry Barbecue Sauce	52
Chili Apple Sauce	54
Green Chili Sauce	55
Spicy Mole Sauce	56
Mexican Tomato Sauce	58
Red Chili Sauce	59
Red Bell Pepper Sauce	60
Roasted Garlic Sauce	61

The Southwest Pantry

I guess if you are under thirty years of age, you might not know what a pantry actually is. So, for educational purposes only, here is Pantry 101. A long, long time ago in a galaxy far, far way, there was a room off the kitchen in many homes which was used for food storage. This room was usually in the north corner of the house since the north was presumed to be the coldest spot. During this time, almost all condiments were made in the kitchen and were stored in bottles or jars. For safekeeping, they were kept in the pantry, as it was cold and usually dark—two important elements in naturally preserving food before there was this thing called "refrigeration."

The pantry, however, was not used for meats, beverages, or produce. Those staples of the kitchen had their own lovely little quarters. The meat was kept in the "larder." The beverages were kept in the "buttery." The produce was kept in the "root cellar."

Now let us take a look at the pantries of today. For the most part, they are called cupboards, and in the average house, they contain a virtual plethora of chemically induced yummies like commercially produced mayonnaise, salsa, mustard, ketchup, and the like. A good idea with a very unhealthy inventory!

In the Southwest, freshness is the key to flavorful dishes, and when it comes to the Southwest Pantry, the head chef is Mother Nature, and the sous chef is you.

In this section, I am not only going to show you how to stock your pantry with the most popular condiments from the Southwest, I am going to show you how to do it naturally. No more chemicals! No more preservatives! Just pure and unadulterated natural flavor. Even better from an economical point, in the long run, this simple little section will end up saving you a lot of money at the supermarket. By the time you have finished having fun in The Southwest Pantry, you will have a pantry every Southwest eatery on the face of this earth will envy.

The Southwest Pantry will give you one of our favorite Southwest snacks: homemade tortilla chips. And due to the fact that there are a few varieties, you can make your favorite nachos a few nights in a row and not be bored. You will also have a bevy of glazes, ketchups, mustards, mayonnaises, marinades, flavored oils, relishes, dry rubs, sauces (all of which are perfect for grilling), and what would a Southwest pantry be without a multitude of different salsas!

If you're not hungry now, you will be by the time you've finished "relishing" the recipes from The Southwest Pantry!

Southwest Chili Chips

Ingredients

peanut or vegetable oil, for frying

24 corn tortillas, cut into
   8 triangles each

1½ Tbs. chili powder

2 tsp. chipotle chili powder

½ tsp. dried oregano, crumbled

¾ tsp. ground cumin

2 tsp. salt

¼ tsp. cayenne pepper

··· Note ···

If making these ahead of time, store in a large brown bag and keep in a cool dark place (like the pantry).

Steps

1. In a large pan or skillet, bring enough peanut oil to deep-fry to 350°F on a deep-fry thermometer.

2. In batches, carefully add the tortillas and fry until crisp and golden.

3. Remove the chips with a slotted spoon and place on a paper towel–covered plate to drain off any excess oil.

4. In a medium bowl, whisk the chili powder, chipotle chili powder, oregano, cumin, salt, and cayenne pepper until well blended.

5. Toss the chips with the spice blend and serve.

Casa Tortilla Chips

Ingredients

peanut or vegetable oil, for frying

24 corn tortillas, cut into 8 triangles
each

1 lime, juice and finely grated zest

1 Tbs. salt

1 tsp. ground cumin

··· Note ···

If making these ahead of time, store in a large brown bag and keep in a cool dark place (like the pantry).

Steps

1. In a large pan or skillet, bring enough peanut oil to deep-fry to 350°F on a deep-fry thermometer.

2. In batches, carefully add the tortillas and fry until crisp and golden.

3. Remove the chips with a slotted spoon and place on a paper towel–covered plate to drain off any excess oil.

4. Sprinkle the chips with the lime juice and toss them to evenly coat.

5. In a small bowl, blend the lime zest, salt, and cumin.

6. Toss the chips with the spice blend and serve.

Spicy Plantain Chips

Ingredients

2 pounds plantains, peeled
peanut or vegetable oil, for frying
½ tsp. chili powder
½ tsp. salt
1 tsp. sugar

Steps

1. Slice the plantains on a slant into thin slices.
2. In a large pan or skillet, heat enough oil to deep-fry to 350°F on a deep-fry thermometer.
3. In batches, carefully add the plantains and fry until crisp and golden.
4. Remove the chips with a slotted spoon and place on a paper towel–covered plate to drain off any excess oil.
5. In a small bowl, whisk the chili powder, salt, and sugar until well blended.
6. Toss the plantain chips with the spice blend and serve.

··· Note ···

Store in a large brown bag and keep in a cool dark place (like the pantry). Plantain chips won't stay fresh as long as tortilla chips do.

Whiskey and Maple Glaze

(Makes about 2 cups)

Ingredients

1 cup pure maple syrup (no, you can't
use pancake syrup)
½ cup water
1 cup pure apple cider
¼ tsp. salt
¼ cup bourbon (or whiskey)

··· Note ···
This is a terrific glaze for
ribs and chops.

Steps

1. In a medium saucepan over
   medium heat, stir the maple
   syrup into the water until it
   has dissolved and bring to a
   boil.

2. Stir in the apple cider, bring
   the mixture to a simmer, and
   cook 10 minutes.

3. Remove the pan from the
   heat and stir in the salt and
   bourbon.

4. Let the mixture cool to room
   temperature.

5. Store the glaze in a jar or
   bottle with an airtight lid
   and keep in the pantry until
   ready to use.

Coffee Barbecue Glaze

(Makes about 2 cups)

Ingredients

1 Tbs. olive oil
1 shallot, minced
2 cloves garlic, minced
½ cup brown sugar
2 tsp. molasses
½ tsp. ground cloves
½ tsp. ground nutmeg
½ tsp. ground allspice
½ cup apple cider vinegar
1 cup organic chili puree
1 cup Smoked Chili Ketchup (page 21)
1 cup strong black coffee
½ cup water
1 tsp. salt

Steps

1. In a medium saucepan, heat the oil over medium heat. Add the shallot and garlic and sauté 2 minutes.
2. Stir in the brown sugar, molasses, cloves, nutmeg, and allspice.
3. Stir in the vinegar, making sure to scrape along the bottom of the pan.
4. Stir in the chili puree and Smoked Chili Ketchup and bring the mixture to a simmer.
5. Stir in the coffee, water, and salt and bring to a boil. Reduce the heat to a simmer and cook 20 minutes (it will thicken).
6. Remove the pan from the heat and let cool.
7. Pour the mixture into a food processor and puree.
8. Store the glaze in a jar or bottle with an airtight lid and keep in the pantry until ready to use.

Roasted Garlic Barbecue Glaze

(Makes about 1 cup)

Ingredients

½ cup rice vinegar
½ cup apple cider vinegar
1 Tbs. whole coriander seeds
2 tsp. whole cloves
3 allspice berries
2 Tbs. olive oil
½ white onion, minced
2 heads roasted garlic, peeled and chopped
¼ cup brown sugar
1 Tbs. molasses
½ bottle high quality Mexican beer
1¾ cups Cinnamon Scented Ketchup (page 18)
½ tsp. salt

Steps

1. In a medium saucepan over medium heat, add the rice vinegar, apple cider vinegar, coriander seeds, cloves, and allspice berries and bring to a boil. Cook the mixture until it has reduced by 50 percent.

2. Strain the mixture through a fine sieve and discard the solids. Set the vinegar mixture aside.

3. In a medium sauté pan, heat the olive oil over medium heat. Add the onion and garlic and sauté 5 minutes.

4. Stir in the brown sugar until the sugar has dissolved.

5. Stir in the molasses and beer, bring to a simmer, and cook 30 minutes.

6. Stir in the Cinnamon Scented Ketchup, salt, and the vinegar mixture and cook 15 minutes.

7. Strain the glaze through a fine sieve into a bowl and discard solids. Set the glaze aside to cool.

8. Store the glaze in a jar or bottle with an airtight lid and keep in the pantry until ready to use.

To roast your own garlic is quite simple. Take a full head of garlic (unpeeled), cut off the top (opposite of the root end), exposing the individual cloves, and place it on a piece of foil. Drizzle the garlic with some olive oil and then wrap it in the foil. Place it in a pan and put it into a pre-heated 400°F oven for 35 minutes. Once it is done, the pulp will squeeze right out of the skin!

Spicy Chipotle Glaze

(Makes about 2 cups)

Ingredients

1 cup rice vinegar
1 cup apple cider vinegar
2 Tbs. whole coriander seeds
1 Tbs. whole cloves
6 allspice berries
¼ cup olive oil
1 white onion, chopped
4 cloves garlic, minced
1 cup brown sugar
¼ cup molasses
1 bottle good quality Mexican beer
½ cup pureed chipotle chilies
1¾ cups Smoked Chili Ketchup (page 21)

> ··· Note ···
>
> This is one of the best glazes you will ever use for barbecued chicken or grilling chops—a little "hot" and a little sweet.

Steps

1. In a medium saucepan over medium heat, stir together the rice vinegar, apple cider vinegar, coriander seeds, cloves, and allspice berries. Bring the mixture to a boil and cook until reduced by half.

2. Strain the mixture through a fine sieve, discard the solids, and set the vinegar liquid aside.

3. In a medium sauté pan, heat the olive oil over medium heat. Add the onion and sauté 5 minutes.

4. Add the garlic and brown sugar and stir until the brown sugar dissolves.

5. Stir in the molasses and beer and cook 5 minutes.

6. Stir in the vinegar liquid and pureed chipotles and bring to a boil.

7. Reduce the heat to a simmer and cook 1 hour.

8. Stir in the Smoked Chili Ketchup and cook 10 minutes.

9. Strain the glaze through a fine sieve and discard the solids.

10. Let the glaze cool to room temperature.

11. Store the glaze in a jar or bottle with an airtight lid and keep in the pantry until ready to use.

··· Note ···

You can find wonderful canned organic chipotle chilies at your market; to puree them, just give them a few whirls in the food processor (including the adobo sauce they are packed in).

Sherry and Shallot Apple Cider Glaze

(Makes about 2 cups)

Ingredients

2 cups apple cider
1 cinnamon stick
2 whole cloves
2 allspice berries
15 shallots, minced
½ cup sherry vinegar
1 Tbs. sherry
½ cup Cumin Oil (page 31)
¼ tsp. salt

Steps

1. In a medium saucepan over medium heat, stir together the apple cider, cinnamon stick, cloves, and allspice, bring to a boil, and cook 5 minutes.

2. Remove the saucepan from the heat and stir in the shallots, sherry vinegar, sherry, Cumin Oil, and salt.

3. Let the mixture cool to room temperature.

4. Strain the liquid through a fine sieve and discard the solids.

5. Store the glaze in a jar or bottle with an airtight lid and keep in the pantry until ready to use.

Chili Rojo Mustard

(Makes about 3 cups)

Ingredients

2 Tbs. chili powder

2 Tbs. water

2 cups quality Dijon-style mustard

½ cup Gringo Mayonnaise (page 20)

½ cup Red Chili Sauce (page 59)

4 green onions, minced

2 Tbs. lime juice

¼ tsp. salt

Steps

1. Place all of the ingredients into a large bowl and whisk until creamy and smooth.

2. Spoon the Chili Rojo Mustard into a jar with an airtight lid and refrigerate until ready to use.

Chipotle Mayonnaise

(Makes about 2 cups)

Ingredients

1 egg
1 egg yolk
¼ cup chipotle chili puree
1 clove garlic, minced
1½ cups peanut oil

Steps

1. In a medium bowl, whisk the egg, egg yolk, chipotle puree, and garlic until combined.

2. Begin whisking in the oil by the teaspoon, whisking after each addition, until thickened (emulsified).

3. Once you have about ¼ cup of the oil emulsified, continue whisking in the oil in a slow steady stream until thickened. You can use an electric mixer with the whisk attachment for the final addition of oil, but I never recommend using a food processor to make mayonnaise.

> ··· Note ···
>
> You can find wonderful canned organic chipotle chilies at your market; to puree them, just give them a few whirls in the food processor (including the adobo sauce they are packed in).

Southwest Style Crème Fraîche

(Makes 2 cups)

Ingredients

1 cup heavy cream
1 cup buttermilk

Steps

1. In a medium saucepan over low heat, bring the cream to 98°F.

2. Stir in the buttermilk just until combined.

3. Remove the pan from the heat and let cool to room temperature.

4. Pour the mixture into a jar with an airtight lid and let sit at room temperature 24 hours.

5. Place the Southwest Style Crème Fraîche in the refrigerator until ready to use.

Cinnamon Scented Ketchup

(Makes about 3 cups)

Ingredients

1 Tbs. Cinnamon Oil (page 30)
1 white onion, chopped
½ cup sugar
2 Tbs. ground cinnamon
1 tsp. ground allspice
½ tsp. ground cloves
2 cups apple cider vinegar
12 Roma tomatoes, halved
1 cup apple cider
1 Tbs. salt

Steps

1. In a large sauté pan or skillet, heat the Cinnamon Oil over medium heat. Add the onion and sauté 5 minutes.
2. Stir in the sugar, cinnamon, allspice, and cloves and cook 2 minutes.
3. Stir in the vinegar and bring the mixture to a boil.
4. Add the tomatoes, apple cider, and salt and bring to a boil.
5. Reduce the heat to a simmer and cook 45 minutes.
6. Remove the pan from the heat and let cool.
7. Place the mixture into a food processor and puree.
8. Pour the puree into a saucepan and bring to a simmer. Let the ketchup simmer about 30 minutes until it thickens.
9. Remove the ketchup from the heat and let cool.
10. Spoon the Cinnamon Scented Ketchup into a jar with an airtight lid and refrigerate until ready to use.

Maple Dill Mustard

(Makes 1½ cups)

Ingredients

½ cup pure maple syrup (no, you can't use pancake syrup)
1 cup quality Dijon-style mustard
2 Tbs. minced dill
1 Tbs. pureed chipotle peppers

Steps

1. In a medium bowl, whisk the maple syrup, Dijon mustard, dill, and chipotle peppers until smooth.
2. Place the Maple Dill Mustard into a jar with an airtight lid and store in the pantry.

··· Note ···

You can find wonderful canned organic chipotle chilies at your market; to puree them, just give them a few whirls in the food processor (including the adobo sauce they are packed in).

Gringo Mayonnaise

(Makes about 1 cup)

Ingredients

1 egg yolk

1½ tsp. lime juice

1 tsp. red wine vinegar

½ tsp. Dijon-style mustard

½ tsp. salt

¾ cup corn oil (or you can use any type
of oil)

Steps

1. In a medium bowl, whisk the
   egg yolk, lime juice, vinegar,
   mustard, and salt.

2. Begin whisking the oil into
   the mixture by ½ teaspoon
   portions until you've used
   up about ¼ cup of the oil.
   This will give you the proper
   emulsification to hold the
   mayonnaise together.

3. Continue to whisk in the
   remaining oil in a slow
   stream. Continue whisking
   until thickened.

4. Spoon into a bowl and chill
   until ready to use.

··· Note ···

I would never recommend
making a mayonnaise
in a food processor or
electric mixer. For proper
mayonnaise, you need
perfect emulsification of
the oil, and a machine can't
give you that.

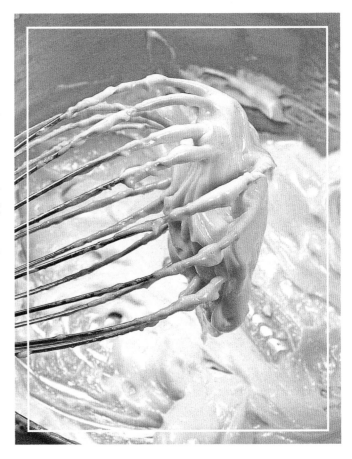

Smoked Chili Ketchup

(Makes about 3 cups)

Ingredients

1 Tbs. Chili Oil (page 29)
1 white onion, chopped
2 tsp. ground cumin
1 Tbs. dried oregano, crumbled
½ cup sugar
1 cup rice vinegar
½ cup Red Chili Sauce (page 59)
¼ cup organic chipotle chilies
8 Roma tomatoes, quartered
2 Tbs. chopped cilantro
1 Tbs. salt

> ··· Note ···
> Chipotle chilies are a smoked jalapeño pepper, thus the name of this ketchup.

Steps

1. In a medium sauté pan, heat the Chili Oil over medium heat. Add the onion and sauté 5 minutes.
2. Stir in the cumin, oregano, and sugar until the sugar has dissolved.
3. Stir in the vinegar, making sure to scrape the bottom of the pan (deglazing).
4. Stir in the Red Chili Sauce, chipotle chilies, tomatoes, cilantro, and salt and bring to a boil.
5. Reduce the heat to a simmer and cook 1 hour.
6. Remove the pan from the heat and let cool.
7. Place the contents into a food processor, in batches if necessary, and puree.
8. Pour the puree into a saucepan and bring to a simmer over medium heat. Let the ketchup cook for about 30 minutes until thickened.
9. Remove the ketchup from the heat and let cool.
10. Pour the Smoked Chili Ketchup into a jar or bottle with an airtight lid and keep in the pantry until ready to use.

Serrano Chili Mayonnaise

(Makes about 3 cups)

Ingredients

10 serrano chili peppers
1 egg
1 egg yolk
1 Tbs. lime juice
1 Tbs. minced cilantro
1½ tsp. salt
2 cups peanut oil

Steps

1. Place the whole serrano peppers over an open flame and char them. Don't worry about burning them because that is exactly what you want to do. If you have an electric range, place them under the broiler.

2. Once the peppers are charred, place them in a brown paper bag and tightly close the bag. Let them rest 15 minutes (they will be steaming themselves in the bag). If you don't have a paper bag, place them beneath a heavy, upside-down bowl.

3. Remove the peppers from the bag and scrape off the skins. The skins will basically slide off the peppers.

4. Chop the peppers. If you want a "less hot" mayonnaise, remove the seeds.

5. Into a food processor, add the chopped serrano peppers, egg, egg yolk, lime juice, cilantro, and salt and puree.

6. Strain the puree through a fine sieve and discard any solids.

7. Spoon the puree into a large bowl and begin whisking in the oil one teaspoon at a time until you've used up about ¼ cup of the oil. Then continue whisking in the remaining oil in a slow, steady stream until it has thickened. This will give you the proper emulsification to hold the mayonnaise together. You can use an electric mixer with a whisk attachment for the final addition of the oil. I never recommend using a food processor to make mayonnaise.

8. Spoon into a bowl and refrigerate until ready to use.

Gin and Juniper Berry Marinade

(Makes about 2 cups)

Ingredients

12 juniper berries, cracked
½ cup gin
½ white onion, minced
1 carrot, minced
1 stalk celery, minced
1 Tbs. rosemary, minced
3 cloves garlic, minced
4 black peppercorns, cracked
2 dried bay leaves, crumbled
1 lime, juice and finely grated
    zest

Steps

1. In a medium bowl, whisk together the juniper berries, gin, white onion, carrot, celery, rosemary, garlic, black peppercorns, bay leaf, lime juice, and lime zest.

2. Spoon the Gin and Juniper Berry Marinade into a jar with an airtight lid and place in the pantry until ready to use.

··· Note ···

To crack juniper berries, simply place them under a plate or flat object and press down with some pressure. To crack black peppercorns, simply give them a slight wallop with a rolling pin.

··· Note ···

This is a very strong marinade, so use sparingly. It's one of my favorites for grilling chicken

Citrus Basil Marinade

(Makes about 2½ cups)

Ingredients

1 cup minced pineapple (if using canned,
   do NOT include the syrup)
1 cup fresh orange juice
¼ cup rice vinegar
2 Tbs. minced basil
¼ cup Lemon Oil (page 32)
1 serrano pepper, minced
¼ tsp. salt

> ··· Note ···
> This is a wonderful marinade
> for both fish and pork.

Steps

1. Into a medium non-aluminum bowl, combine the pineapple, orange juice, rice vinegar, basil, Lemon Oil, serrano pepper, and salt.

2. Pour the Citrus Basil Marinade into a jar or bottle with an airtight lid and keep in the pantry until ready to use.

> ··· Note ···
> You never want to use an aluminum bowl when preparing citrus, or the color and flavor of the citrus will become distorted.

Spicy Lime and Cilantro Marinade

(Makes about ¼ cup)

Ingredients

2 Tbs. lime juice
2 tsp. Cumin Oil (page 31)
1 Tbs. rice vinegar
1 Tbs. minced cilantro
1 serrano pepper, minced
1 tsp. honey

> ··· Note ···
>
> To make this Spicy Lime and Cilantro Marinade less "hot," remove the seeds from the serrano pepper before adding it to the marinade.

Steps

1. In a non-aluminum bowl, stir together the lime juice, Cumin Oil, rice vinegar, cilantro, serrano pepper, and sugar until the sugar has dissolved.

2. Pour the Spicy Lime and Cilantro Marinade into a jar or bottle with an airtight lid and keep in the pantry until ready to use.

> ··· Note ···
>
> This is a rather potent marinade. Due to the high acidity, do not marinate over 30 minutes or it will begin to naturally "cook" the meat.

Sweet Pepper and Cilantro Marinade

(Makes about 1¾ cups)

Ingredients

1 sweet red bell pepper, seeded and minced

2 Tbs. minced cilantro

2 serrano peppers, minced

1 lemon, juice and finely grated zest

1 lime, juice only

1 orange, juice and finely grated zest

½ cup Basil Oil (page 28)

½ tsp. salt

Steps

1. In a medium non-aluminum bowl, stir together the sweet pepper, cilantro, serrano peppers, lemon juice, lemon zest, lime juice, orange juice, orange zest, Basil Oil, and salt.

2. Pour the Sweet Pepper and Cilantro Marinade into a jar or bottle and keep in the pantry until ready to use.

··· Note ···

The best way to get finely grated zest (the colorful part of the citrus skin) is to use a plane grater. You can find them at all kitchenware stores. If you are not using organic citrus, scrub the fruit before zesting.

··· Note ···

Due to the high acidity, do not marinate over 30 minutes or it will begin to naturally "cook" the meat.

Tangerine and Tequila Marinade

(Makes about 2 cups)

Ingredients

¼ cup sugar

½ cup rice vinegar

1 tsp. Mexican Tomato Sauce (page 58)

8 tangerines, juice and finely grated zest from each

¼ cup tequila

1 Tbs. lime juice

1 Tbs. Chili Oil (page 29)

1 Tbs. minced mint

¼ tsp. salt

> ··· Note ···
>
> This is one of my favorite marinades for chicken. You can also use this as a glaze when grilling.

Steps

1. In a medium saucepan over medium heat, stir the sugar, rice vinegar, and Mexican Tomato Sauce until the sugar dissolves and then bring the mixture to a boil.

2. Stir in the tangerine juice and zest and remove the pan from the heat.

3. Stir in the tequila, lime juice, Chili Oil, mint, and salt.

4. Let cool to room temperature.

5. Pour the Tangerine and Tequila Marinade into a jar or bottle with an airtight cap and keep in the pantry until ready to use.

Basil Oil

(Makes 3 cups)

Ingredients

1 cup basil leaves, coarsely chopped
12 cloves garlic, flattened
3 cups extra virgin olive oil

Steps

1. In a jar with an airtight lid, combine the basil, garlic, and olive oil and shake well.

2. Place the Basil Oil in the pantry for 24 hours, shaking the contents a few times.

3. Strain the Basil Oil through a fine sieve into a bottle with an airtight lid. Discard the solids.

4. Store in the pantry until ready to use.

···Note···

Place a basil leaf or two in the bottle for decoration and to show you it is Basil Oil.

···Note···

To flatten garlic is simple. Peel the garlic and then, using the flat side of a knife, give it a whack! It will flatten out and the essential oil of the garlic will be released.

Chili Oil

(Makes 2 cups)

Ingredients

2 cups vegetable oil
½ cup dried chili flakes

Steps

1. In a medium saucepan, heat the vegetable oil over medium heat. You only want it to get to about 100°F.

2. Into the oil, stir the chili flakes and cook 2 minutes.

3. Remove the pan from the heat and let cool to room temperature.

4. Pour the Chili Oil into a bottle with an airtight lid (including the chili flakes) and let sit in the pantry a few days, shaking the bottle a few times a day.

5. Strain the oil through a fine sieve and discard the solids.

6. Pour back into a bottle with an airtight lid and keep in the pantry until ready to use.

··· Note ···

Place a small whole red chili or two in the bottle for decoration and to show you it is Chili Oil.

Cinnamon Oil

(Makes 2 cups)

Ingredients

2 cups vegetable oil
5 cinnamon sticks, broken into pieces

Steps

1. In a small saucepan, heat the vegetable oil over medium heat. You want it to get to about 100°F.

2. Add the cinnamon and cook 2 minutes.

3. Remove the pan from the heat and let cool to room temperature.

4. Pour the Cinnamon Oil into a bottle with an airtight lid and place in the pantry for a few days, shaking the bottle a few times a day.

5. Strain the oil through a fine sieve and discard any solids.

6. Pour the oil back into a bottle with an airtight lid, add a few whole cinnamon sticks, and keep in the pantry until ready to use.

Cumin Oil

(Makes 3 cups)

Ingredients

3 cups olive oil
¼ cup cumin seeds
2 Tbs. dried oregano, crumbled

Steps

1. In a small saucepan, heat the olive oil over medium heat. You want it to get to about 125°F.
2. Add the cumin seeds and oregano and cook 3 minutes.
3. Remove the pan from heat and let cool to room temperature.
4. Pour the oil into a bottle with an airtight lid and place in the pantry 48 hours, shaking the bottle a few times a day.
5. Strain the Cumin Oil through a fine sieve and discard the solids.
6. Pour the Cumin Oil back into a bottle with an airtight lid, add about a tablespoon of cumin seeds, and keep in the pantry until ready to use.

Lemon Oil

(Makes 2 cups)

Ingredients
2 cups peanut oil
4 lemons, zest only

Steps
1. In a small saucepan, heat the peanut oil over medium heat. You only want it to get to about 100°F.
2. Add the lemon zest and cook 1 minute.
3. Remove the pan from the heat and let cool to room temperature.
4. Pour the Lemon Oil into a bottle with an airtight lid and place in the pantry 36 hours, shaking it a few times each day.
5. Strain the Lemon Oil through a fine sieve and discard the solids.
6. Pour the Lemon Oil back into a bottle with an airtight lid and keep in the pantry until ready to use.

··· Note ···

You only want to use peanut oil for Lemon Oil as peanut oil has no flavor, thus your Lemon Oil will always taste fresh.

··· Note ···

You might have noticed that other infused oil recipes in this cookbook recommend placing a piece of the infused item into the bottle for easy identification as well as decoration. However, I do not recommend doing this for the Lemon Oil because the lemon might possibly get moldy. Just find a way to label this on the outside of the bottle if you need a reminder of what's inside.

Santa Fe Ginger Relish

(Makes about 2 cups, depending on size of peppers)

Ingredients

1 Tbs. Chili Oil (page 29)

2 sweet red bell peppers, seeded and chopped

2 sweet yellow bell peppers, seeded and chopped

1 Tbs. grated ginger

½ cup raw honey

½ tsp. salt

1 cup apple cider vinegar

Steps

1. In a medium sauté pan, heat the Chili Oil over medium heat. Add the red peppers, yellow peppers, and ginger and sauté 5 minutes.

2. Stir in the honey, salt, and apple cider vinegar and simmer 15 minutes.

3. Remove the pan from the heat and let cool to room temperature.

4. Spoon the Santa Fe Ginger Relish into a jar with an airtight lid and refrigerate until ready to use.

Five Onion Relish

(Makes about 3 cups)

Ingredients

¼ cup Lemon Oil (page 32)
1 white onion, thinly sliced
1 red onion, thinly sliced
1 bunch (about 5 stems) green onions, chopped
1 leek, tender white part only, chopped
4 cloves garlic, thinly sliced
½ tsp. honey
½ tsp. chili powder
¼ tsp. salt
½ cup sherry vinegar
1 Tbs. minced thyme
¼ tsp. ground black pepper

Steps

1. In a medium saucepan, heat the Lemon Oil over medium heat. Add the white onion, red onion, green onions, leek, and garlic and sauté 10 minutes.

2. Stir in the honey, chili powder, and salt and cook 5 minutes.

3. Stir in the vinegar and cook until the mixture has thickened.

4. Remove the pan from the heat and stir in the thyme and black pepper.

5. Let cool to room temperature.

6. Spoon the Five Onion Relish into a jar with an airtight lid and refrigerate until ready to use.

Mint Breeze Mango Relish

(Makes about 2 cups, depending on size of mangoes)

Ingredients

1 Tbs. Lemon Oil (page 32)
2 shallots, minced
1 Tbs. grated ginger
2 mangoes, peeled, pitted, and diced
½ cup raw honey
1 Tbs. chili powder
2 Tbs. raspberry vinegar
½ cup chopped mint
1 tsp. salt

Steps

1. In a medium sauté pan, heat the Lemon Oil over medium heat. Add the shallots and ginger and sauté 3 minutes.

2. Stir in the mangoes, honey, and chili powder and cook 5 minutes.

3. Stir in the raspberry vinegar, making sure to scrape the bottom of the pan (deglazing).

4. Remove the pan from the heat and stir in the mint and salt.

5. Let cool to room temperature.

6. Spoon the Mint Breeze Mango Relish into a jar with an airtight lid and refrigerate until ready to serve.

Bourbon Peach Relish

(Makes about 3 cups, depending on the size of the peaches)

Ingredients

1 Tbs. butter

1 white onion, thinly sliced

4 peaches (white or yellow variety), peeled, pitted, and sliced

½ cup bourbon

½ cup water

½ cup brown sugar

1 orange, juice only

1 lemon, juice only

1 Tbs. molasses

1 cinnamon stick

½ tsp. salt

Steps

1. In a medium saucepan, melt the butter over medium heat. Add the onion and sauté 5 minutes.

2. Add the peaches and cook 5 minutes.

3. Remove the pan from the heat and stir in the bourbon, water, brown sugar, orange juice, lemon juice, molasses, cinnamon stick, and salt.

4. Place the pan back on the heat. Bring to a simmer and cook 10 minutes (it will thicken).

5. Remove the pan from the heat and let cool to room temperature.

6. Spoon the Bourbon Peach Relish into a jar with an airtight lid and refrigerate until ready to use.

··· Note ···

When adding alcohol to a pan, always remove it from the heat to avoid a flame-up.

Ancho Chili Butter Rub

(Makes about 2 cups)

Ingredients

4 dried ancho chilies
1 pound butter, softened
1 Tbs. brown sugar
½ tsp. ground allspice
1 orange, finely grated zest only
1 tsp. chili powder
½ tsp. salt

Steps

1. Bring a large pot of water to a boil. Add the dried chilies and bring back to a boil.

2. Remove the pot from the heat, place a lid on it, and let the chilies soak for at least 2 hours.

3. Drain the chilies and discard the water. Coarsely chop the peppers, place into a food processor, and puree.

4. In a mixer with the paddle attachment, beat the butter, brown sugar, allspice, orange zest, chili powder, salt, and pureed chilies until smooth.

5. Spoon the Ancho Chili Butter Rub into a bowl, cover with plastic wrap, and chill until ready to use.

··· Note ···

Not only is this great spread on grilled meats, but use it to fry eggs and sauté vegetables! It's a little spicy but not "hot."

Cumin and Black Pepper Rub

(Makes about ¾ cup)

Ingredients

¼ cup cumin seeds
2 Tbs. dried oregano
1 Tbs. black peppercorns
¼ tsp. salt
½ tsp. sugar

Steps

1. In a small sauté pan over medium heat, add the cumin seeds, oregano, and black peppercorns and toast 2 minutes.

2. Into a spice or coffee grinder, place the toasted cumin seeds, oregano, and black peppercorn; add salt and sugar and grind until smooth. If you want it coarser, use a mortar and pestle.

3. Spoon the Cumin and Black Pepper Rub into a jar with an airtight lid and keep in the pantry until ready to use.

> ··· Note ···
> Toasting the spices bring out their essential oils and makes this blend not only tastier, but also gives off an incredible aroma.

Picante Chili Rub

(Makes about 1 cup)

Ingredients

2 Tbs. pureed chipotle chilies
1 Tbs. dried oregano, crumbled
¾ cup chili powder
1 Tbs. sugar
1 tsp. salt

··· Note ···
This is hot! Use sparingly.

Steps

1. In a medium non-aluminum bowl, whisk the pureed chipotle chilies, oregano, chili powder, sugar, and salt until smooth.

2. Spoon the Picante Chili Rub into a small jar with an airtight lid and refrigerate until ready to serve.

··· Note ···
You can find wonderful canned organic chipotle chilies at your market; to puree them, just give them a few whirls in the food processor (including the adobo sauce they are packed in).

Red Chili Salsa

(Makes about 2 cups)

Ingredients

½ pound dried ancho chilies
4 cloves garlic, peeled and whole
1 tsp. salt
1 Tbs. dried oregano, crumbled

··· Note ···

This is spicy but not "hot"—a perfect salsa for tacos and nachos.

Steps

1. Bring a large pot of water to a boil. Add the dried chilies and bring back to a boil.

2. Remove the pot from the heat, place a lid on it and let the chilies soak for at least 2 hours.

3. Coarsely chop the chilies and place them into a food processor. Add a little of the soaking water as needed and puree the chilies. You are looking for the consistency of a thick sauce.

4. Into the food processor, add the garlic, salt, and oregano and puree.

5. Spoon the Red Chili Salsa into a small jar with an airtight lid and refrigerate until ready to use.

Citrus Tequila Salsa

(Makes about 5 cups, depending on size of fruit)

Ingredients

1 pineapple, diced
1 grapefruit, sectioned and diced
2 oranges, sectioned and diced
2 limes, sectioned and diced
1 lemon, sectioned and diced
2 Tbs. minced cilantro
2 Tbs. honey
½ tsp. salt
1 tsp. ground cayenne pepper
¼ cup tequila

··· Note ···

To section citrus fruit simply means to remove the rind and then cut out the fruit from between the membranes (white pithy part). This also makes for a great fruit salad when topped with a dollop of Southwest Style Crème Fraîche (page 17).

Steps

1. In a large non-aluminum bowl, combine the pineapple, grapefruit, oranges, limes, lemon, cilantro, honey, salt, and cayenne pepper and gently toss to coat.

2. Let sit at room temperature 30 minutes.

3. Stir in the tequila.

4. Spoon the Citrus Tequila Salsa into a jar with an airtight lid and refrigerate until ready to use.

Green Chili Salsa

(Makes about 3 cups)

Ingredients

2 Tbs. Basil Oil (page 28)

½ white onion, minced

1 clove garlic, minced

8 jalapeño chilies, charred, peeled, and diced

½ tsp. ground cumin

½ tsp. dried oregano, crumbled

2 cups water

1 Tbs. minced cilantro

1 tsp. salt

> ··· Note ···
>
> To char the jalapeño peppers, place them over an open flame (or under the broiler) until they char (burn) all over. Then place them in a paper bag for 15 minutes (they will steam themselves). Take them out, and their skins will just slide off

Steps

1. In a medium sauté pan, heat the Basil Oil over medium heat. Add the onion and sauté 5 minutes.

2. Add the garlic, chilies, cumin, and oregano and sauté 3 minutes.

3. Stir in the water and bring the salsa to a boil. Reduce the heat to a simmer and cook 20 minutes.

4. Remove the pan from the heat and let cool to room temperature.

5. Stir in the cilantro and salt.

6. Spoon the Green Chili Salsa into a jar with an airtight lid and store in the refrigerator until ready to use.

Hotter Than Hell Salsa

(Makes about 2 cups)

Ingredients

2 habanero chilies, diced (good idea to wear gloves when dicing habaneros)

1 sweet red bell pepper, seeded and diced

1 mango, peeled, pitted, and diced

2 green onions, minced

2 Tbs. lime juice

2 Tbs. dark rum

1 tsp. rice vinegar

1 tsp. grated ginger

1 tsp. salt

1 tsp. raw honey

Steps

1. In a large non-aluminum bowl, combine the habanero chilies, sweet red bell pepper, mango, green onions, lime juice, dark rum, rice vinegar, ginger, salt, and honey.

2. Let sit at room temperature 30 minutes.

3. Spoon the Hotter Than Hell Salsa into a jar with an airtight lid and refrigerate until ready to use.

··· Note ···

This is HOT. Habanero chilies are a very hot pepper. If you have gastrointestinal problems, this salsa is not a good idea. Instead, you can make this with jalapeño or serrano chilies, which are much less hot

Mango Jicama Salsa

(Makes about 3 cups)

Ingredients

1 small jicama, peeled and diced

1 mango, peeled, pitted, and diced

½ sweet red bell pepper, seeded and diced

½ sweet yellow bell pepper, seeded and diced

1 green onion, minced

1 serrano pepper, diced

2 Tbs. lime juice

1 Tbs. minced cilantro

1 Tbs. minced mint

½ tsp. grated ginger

2 tsp. red wine vinegar

1 Tbs. Cumin Oil (page 31)

1 tsp. sugar

··· Note ···

Jicama is a root vegetable with a wonderful slightly sweet freshness and can be found at most supermarkets in the produce section.

Steps

1. In a medium non-aluminum bowl, combine the jicama, mango, red bell pepper, yellow bell pepper, green onion, serrano pepper, lime juice, cilantro, mint, and ginger. Let sit at room temperature for 30 minutes.

2. Stir in the red wine vinegar, Cumin Oil, and sugar.

3. Spoon the Mango Jicama Salsa into a jar with an airtight lid and refrigerate until ready to use.

Multi-Melon Salsa

(Makes about 5 cups, depending on size of melons)

Ingredients

1 cantaloupe, peeled and diced

1 honeydew melon, peeled and diced

1 sweet red bell pepper, seeded and diced

2 serrano peppers, minced

2 Tbs. minced mint

1 Tbs. apple cider vinegar

2 Tbs. lime juice

1 Tbs. raw honey

··· Note ···

The best way to peel any large melon is to first cut the melon into quarters and then, with a sharp paring knife, simply remove the rind from the pulp (fruit).

Steps

1. In a large non-aluminum bowl, combine the cantaloupe, honeydew, red bell pepper, serrano peppers, and mint and let sit at room temperature for 30 minutes.

2. Stir in the apple cider vinegar, lime juice, and raw honey.

3. Spoon the Multi-Melon Salsa into a jar with an airtight lid and refrigerate until ready to use.

Pineapple Salsa

(Makes about 4 cups, depending on size of pineapple)

Ingredients

1 pineapple, cut into ¼-inch-thick round slices
½ sweet red bell pepper, seeded and diced
2 jalapeño peppers, minced
2 Tbs. orange juice
1 Tbs. lime juice
1 Tbs. minced cilantro
1 Tbs. raw honey

Steps

1. Cut each of the pineapple slices in half, making sure the core is removed and discarded (you'll end up with crescent-shaped pieces).

2. Heat a non-stick pan over medium heat. Place the pineapple into the pan and dry-fry until it starts to get some color. This is bringing out the natural sugars in the pineapple, and the darkness you'll see is the caramelization of the natural sugar.

3. Remove the pineapple from the pan and chop or dice it.

4. In a large non-aluminum bowl, combine the pineapple, red bell pepper, jalapeño peppers, orange juice, lime juice, cilantro, and honey.

5. Let sit at room temperature for 30 minutes.

6. Spoon the Pineapple Salsa into a jar with an airtight lid and refrigerate until ready to use.

Salsa Fresca

(Makes about 4 cups)

Ingredients

½ white onion, minced

8 Roma tomatoes, diced

2 serrano peppers, minced

2 Tbs. minced cilantro

1 tsp. raw honey

¼ cup quality Mexican beer (go ahead and drink the rest of the bottle)

1 tsp. salt

1 Tbs. lime juice

··· Note ···

For best taste result, let the Salsa Fresca come to room temperature before serving it. About 30 minutes out of the refrigerator is perfect.

Steps

1. In a medium non-aluminum bowl, combine the onion, tomatoes, serrano peppers, cilantro, and raw honey. Let the mixture sit at room temperature 30 minutes.

2. Stir in the beer, salt, and lime juice.

3. Spoon the Salsa Fresca into a jar with an airtight lid and refrigerate until ready to use.

Sweet Pepper Salsa

(Makes about 1½ cups)

Ingredients

½ sweet red bell pepper, seeded and minced

½ sweet yellow bell pepper, seeded and minced

2 serrano peppers, minced

2 shallots, minced

¼ cup raspberry vinegar

1 tsp. salt

2 Tbs. lime juice

1 tsp. sugar

2 Tbs. Lemon Oil (page 32)

1 green onion, minced

1 Tbs. minced cilantro

Steps

1. In a medium non-aluminum bowl, combine the red bell pepper, yellow bell pepper, serrano peppers, shallots, raspberry vinegar, and salt. Let the mixture sit at room temperature 30 minutes.

2. Stir in the lime juice, sugar, Lemon Oil, green onion, and cilantro.

3. Spoon the Sweet Pepper Salsa into a jar with an airtight lid and refrigerate until ready to use.

Tequila Salsa

(Makes about 3 cups)

Ingredients

2 shallots, minced
1 pound cherry tomatoes, quartered
2 jalapeño peppers, minced
2 Tbs. minced cilantro
2 tsp. raw honey
¼ cup tequila
1 Tbs. lime juice

··· Note ···

You can substitute grape tomatoes for cherry tomatoes. If using grape tomatoes, cut them in half instead of quarters since they are much smaller.

Steps

1. In a medium non-aluminum bowl, combine the shallots, tomatoes, jalapeño peppers, cilantro, honey, tequila, and lime juice. Let the mixture sit at room temperature for 30 minutes.

2. Spoon the Tequila Salsa into a jar with an airtight lid and refrigerate until ready to use.

Tomatillo and Serrano Salsa

(Makes about 4 cups, depending on size of tomatillos)

Ingredients

15 tomatillos, chopped
3 serrano peppers, minced
1 Tbs. honcy
½ cup chopped cilantro
2 tsp. salt
1 cup water, divided
2 Tbs. lime juice
1 avocado, peeled, pitted, and
  diced

Steps

1. Into a food processor, place the tomatillos, serrano peppers, honey, cilantro, salt, and ½ cup water and puree.

2. Pour the puree into a medium non-aluminum bowl and stir in the remaining ½ cup water, lime juice, and avocado.

3. Let the mixture sit at room temperature for 30 minutes.

4. Spoon the Tomatillo and Serrano Salsa into a jar with an airtight lid and refrigerate until ready to use.

··· Note ···

Fresh tomatillos will have a natural paper-like husk over their skin. Simply remove this skin and discard before cutting the tomatillos.

Salsa Tropical

(Makes about 4 cups)

Ingredients

½ pineapple, diced
1 mango, peeled, pitted, and diced
1 papaya, peeled, seeded and diced
½ sweet red bell pepper, diced
1 Tbs. minced mint
1 shallot, minced
2 Tbs. orange juice
1 Tbs. lime juice
½ tsp. grated ginger
½ tsp. salt
1 Tbs. raw honey

Steps

1. In a large non-aluminum bowl, combine the pineapple, mango, papaya, red bell pepper, mint, and shallot. Let the mixture sit at room temperature for 30 minutes.

2. Stir in the orange juice, lime juice, ginger, salt, and honey.

3. Spoon the Salsa Tropical into a jar with an airtight lid and refrigerate until ready to use.

··· Note ···

There are a few varieties of papaya now available in most markets. Unless otherwise noted in the recipe, the only papayas I use are the smaller varieties usually from Hawaii or South America.

Cherry Barbecue Sauce

(Makes about 3 cups)

Ingredients

1 cup rice vinegar
1 cup apple cider vinegar
1 tsp. whole allspice berries
1 tsp. whole coriander seeds
2 Tbs. Lemon Oil (page 32)
½ white onion, minced
2 cloves garlic, minced
½ cup brown sugar
2 Tbs. molasses
1 cup dried cherries
2 cups ancho chili puree
1¾ cups Smoked Chili Ketchup (page 21)
1 cup water
1 tsp. salt
2 Tbs. Cumin Oil (page 31)

Steps

1. In a small saucepan over medium heat, whisk together the rice vinegar, apple cider vinegar, allspice, and coriander until the mixture comes to a boil. Reduce the heat to a simmer and cook 10 minutes.

2. Remove the pan from heat and strain the mixture through a fine sieve and discard the solids. Set aside vinegar mixture.

3. In a large sauté pan, heat the Lemon Oil over medium heat. Add the onion and garlic and sauté 5 minutes.

4. Stir in the brown sugar and molasses until the brown sugar dissolves.

5. Stir in the vinegar mixture, dried cherries, ancho chili puree, Smoked Chili Ketchup, and water and bring to a boil.

6. Reduce the heat to a simmer and cook 20 minutes.

7. Remove the pan from heat and let cool 5 minutes.

8. Spoon the mixture into a food processor, add the salt, and puree.

9. Strain the puree through a fine sieve and discard the solids. Set aside the sauce mixture.

10. In the same sauté pan, heat the Cumin Oil over medium heat.

11. Stir in the pureed sauce and cook 5 minutes.

12. Remove from heat and let cool to room temperature.

13. Pour the Cherry Barbecue Sauce into a bottle or jar with an airtight container and store in the pantry until ready to use.

··· Note ···

You can make your own chili puree! Bring a large pot of water to a boil. Add the dried chilies and bring back to a boil. Remove the pot from the heat, place a lid on it, and let the chilies soak for at least 2 hours. Drain the chilies and discard the water. Coarsely chop the peppers, place into a food processor with a little salt, apple cider vinegar, and water, and puree. You want it to be rather thick.

Chili Apple Sauce

(Makes about 4 cups)

Ingredients

1 Tbs. butter

4 Granny Smith apples, peeled, cored, and chopped

2 Anaheim peppers, chopped

2 serrano peppers, chopped

¼ cup sugar

1 tsp. ground cinnamon

1 cup apple cider

1 Tbs. lemon juice

1 tsp. dried oregano, crumbled

½ tsp. salt

··· Note ···

Due to the way this sauce is cooked, I would only recommend using Granny Smith (green apples). Other apple varieties contain too much liquid, and it ruins the taste and texture of the sauce.

Steps

1. In a large sauté pan, melt the butter over medium heat. Add the apples, Anaheim peppers, and serrano peppers and sauté 5 minutes.

2. Stir in the sugar, cinnamon, apple cider, lemon juice, oregano, and salt and bring to a boil.

3. Reduce the heat to a simmer and cook 10 minutes. You will want most of the liquid to evaporate.

4. Remove the pan from heat and let cool.

5. Place the mixture into a food processor and puree.

6. Spoon the Chili Apple Sauce into a jar with an airtight lid and refrigerate until ready to use.

Green Chili Sauce

(Makes about 5 cups)

Ingredients

20 Anaheim peppers
4 jalapeño peppers
6 cloves garlic, chopped
4 cups water
2 tsp. dried oregano, crumbled
1 tsp. ground cumin
2 tsp. salt

··· Note ···

Many people will heat this sauce before using it. Though, if using for tacos, it is much better straight from the refrigerator.

Steps

1. Char the Anaheim and jalapeño peppers over an open flame (or under the broiler). You want them completely charred (skins burned). Place them in a large brown bag and let them sit (steam) 15 minutes.

2. Remove the peppers and scrape off the skins.

3. Into a food processor, place the peppers, garlic, water, oregano, cumin, and salt.

4. Pulse the food processor a few times. You don't really want it pureed; you want some texture.

5. Spoon the Green Chili Sauce into a jar with an airtight lid and refrigerate until ready to use.

Spicy Mole Sauce

(Makes about 4 cups)

Ingredients

8 cups boiling water
10 dried ancho chilies
8 dried mulato chilies
6 dried pasilla chilies
½ cup dried cherries
4 tomatillos
5 Roma tomatoes
⅓ cup pumpkin seeds
½ cup almonds
1 Tbs. Chili Oil (page 29)
2 corn tortillas, dried (stale) and cut into strips
6 cloves garlic, peeled and whole
2 cups cold water
2 tsp. ground cinnamon
4 whole cloves
½ tsp. ground black pepper
6 allspice berries
1 tsp. salt
3 Tbs. Cinnamon Oil (page 30)
6 ounces unsweetened chocolate, melted

Steps

1. Bring 8 cups of water to a boil. Add all three types of dried chilies and the dried cherries; bring back to a boil.

2. Remove the pot from the heat, place a lid on it, and let the chilies and cherries soak for 2 hours.

3. Char the tomatillos and tomatoes over an open flame (or under the broiler).

4. Put the charred tomatillos and tomatoes into the chili-and-cherry water for a minute, then remove and scrape off their skins. Leave the chilies and cherries in the water.

5. In a medium sauté pan over medium heat, combine the pumpkin seeds, almonds, and Chili Oil and cook 5 minutes (this will release the essential oils of the nuts and seeds).

6. Into a food processor, place the tomatillos, tomatoes, pumpkin seeds, almonds, and dried tortillas and puree.

7. Remove the chilies from the water and coarsely chop. Remove cherries from the water.

8. Into the food processor place the peppers, cherries, garlic, cold water, cinnamon, cloves, black pepper, allspice, and salt and puree.

9. Pour the puree into the sauté pan and cook over medium heat 30 minutes.

10. Remove the mixture from the heat and strain through a fine sieve, discarding the solids.

11. Clean out the sauté pan. Place back on medium heat and heat the Cinnamon Oil.

12. Pour the strained puree into the sauté pan and cook 10 minutes.

13. Stir the melted chocolate into the sauce and remove from heat to cool.

14. Once cooled, spoon the Spicy Mole Sauce into a jar with an airtight lid and refrigerate until ready to use.

··· Note ···

This sauce will thicken as it cools.

Mexican Tomato Sauce

(Makes about 3 cups)

Ingredients

8 Roma tomatoes
4 cloves garlic, chopped
4 large red jalapeño peppers, chopped
¼ cup tequila
¼ cup chopped cilantro
1 Tbs. lime juice
¼ tsp. salt

Steps

1. Char the tomatoes over an open flame (or under the broiler).

2. Place the tomatoes into a bowl of ice water and soak for about a minute. Remove them and scrape off their skins.

3. Chop the tomatoes and place them into a food processor with the garlic, peppers, tequila, cilantro, lime juice, and salt.

4. Puree the mixture until smooth.

5. Spoon the Mexican Tomato Sauce into a jar with an airtight lid and refrigerate until ready to use.

··· Note ···

If you cannot find Roma tomatoes at your supermarket, you can use plum tomatoes as they are essentially the same thing. You don't want to strain this sauce, as you want the texture of the tomatoes and peppers. Also, this won't be the red tomato sauce you're used to. This is natural: no preservatives or coloring.

Red Chili Sauce

(Makes about 3 cups)

Ingredients

8 Roma tomatoes
½ pound dried ancho chilies
4 cups boiling water
1 Tbs. Chili Oil (page 29)
1 white onion, chopped
2 cloves garlic, minced
1 tsp. ground cumin
1 tsp. dried oregano, crumbled
1 tsp. salt
2 Tbs. Basil Oil (page 28)

Steps

1. Char the tomatoes over an open flame (or under the broiler).
2. Place the tomatoes into a bowl of ice water for a minute. Remove the tomatoes and peel off their skin.
3. Chop the tomatoes, place them into a new bowl, and chill.
4. Place the dried chilies in the 4 cups of boiling water. Remove from heat and let them soak 2 hours.
5. Remove the chilies from the water and coarsely chop. Reserve 1 cup of the soaking water.
6. In a medium sauté pan, heat the Chili Oil over medium heat. Add the onion and sauté 5 minutes.
7. Into a food processor, add the tomatoes, chilies, onion, garlic, cumin, oregano, and salt and puree.
8. While the food processor is going, slowly add the reserved chili-soaking liquid.
9. In the sauté pan, heat the Basil Oil over medium heat.
10. Pour the chili sauce into the pan and cook 5 minutes.
11. Remove the pan from the heat and let cool
12. Spoon the Red Chili Sauce into a jar with an airtight lid and refrigerate until ready to use.

Red Bell Pepper Sauce

(Makes about 3 cups)

Ingredients

2 sweet red bell peppers
½ cup Chili Oil (page 29), divided
1 white onion, chopped
2 cloves garlic, minced
2 Tbs. balsamic vinegar
½ cup water
1 Tbs. minced basil
2 tsp. chili powder
1 Tbs. Red Chili Sauce (page 59)
1 tsp. salt

Steps

1. Char the sweet red bell peppers over an open flame (or under the broiler). Once charred, remove from heat and place inside a paper bag for 15 minutes to steam.

2. Remove the peppers from the bag and scrape off the skin. Cut the peppers in half and remove the seeds, then chop the peppers.

3. In a medium sauté pan, heat 2 Tbs. Chili Oil over medium heat. Add the onion and sauté 5 minutes.

4. Into a food processor, add the bell peppers, onion, garlic, vinegar, water, basil, chili powder, and Red Chili Sauce and puree.

5. With the food processor running, add the remaining oil in a steady stream; add the salt.

6. Spoon the Red Bell Pepper Sauce into a jar with an airtight lid and refrigerate until ready to use.

Roasted Garlic Sauce

(Makes about 1 cup)

Ingredients

2 heads roasted garlic
2 Tbs. butter
2 Tbs. Chili Oil (page 29)
2 shallots, thinly sliced
1 cup cream
1 cup chicken stock
½ cup dry sherry
1 Tbs. minced thyme
1 tsp. salt
½ tsp. ground black pepper

> ··· Note ···
> This is a very popular white sauce for pizzas!

Steps

1. Squeeze the pulp from the cloves of garlic into a bowl. Discard the skins.
2. In a medium saucepan, melt the butter into the Chili Oil. Add the shallots and garlic pulp and sauté 5 minutes.
3. Stir in the cream and chicken stock and bring to a simmer (do not let it boil or the cream will separate).
4. Reduce the heat to low and cook 10 minutes.
5. Stir in the sherry and cook 5 minutes.
6. Remove the pan from the heat and stir in the thyme, salt, and pepper.
7. Spoon the sauce into a food processor and puree.
8. Let cool to room temperature.
9. Spoon the Roasted Garlic Sauce into a jar with an airtight lid and refrigerate until ready to use.

> ··· Note ···
> To roast your own garlic is quite simple. Cut off the tops (opposite of the root end), exposing the individual cloves, and place each of the heads of garlic on a piece of foil. Drizzle the garlic with some olive oil and then wrap the foil around each head. Place them on a baking sheet and place into a pre-heated 400°F oven and roast 35 minutes. Once done, pinch the pulp right out of the skins.

The Southwest Kitchen

Meat

Baja Flank Ribs with Tequila and Honey Glaze	64
Whiskey Maple Glazed Ribs	66
Braised Short Ribs	68
Jalapeño Tequila Bombs	70
Kahlúa Country Style Pork Ribs	72
Kahlúa Glazed Flank Ribs	74
Poached Poblano Peppers	76
Port Braised Short Ribs	78
Root Beer Ribs	80
Southwest Grilled Rum Ribs	82
Christmas Ribs	84
Southwest Bacon Burger	86

Poultry

Barbecue Fried Chicken	88
Bourbon Braised Turkey Necks	90
Chicken Española	92
Chicken Merlot	94
Chicken with Cherry Salsa	96
Chicken Zinfandel	98
Frisco Funky Fried Chicken	100
Honey Stung Fried Chicken	102
Kahlúa Braised Chicken	104
Punk'd Chicken	106
Santa Fe Chicken Wings	108
Spiced Southwest Tequila Chicken	110
Skins and 'Shrooms	112
Spicy Kahlúa Chicken	114

Seafood

Paco Shrimp with Peppers	115
Baby Portobellos with Sautéed Shrimp	116
Broiled Salmon with Bourbon Glaze	118
Southwest Crab Cakes	120
Grilled Portobellos with Crab Anglaise	122
Kahlúa Shrimp Azteca	124
Scallops in Mango Butter	126
Sherry Shrimp with Endive	128

Shrimp de la Cancun	130
Santa Ana Shrimp and Snapper	132
Casa Red Snapper	134
Spiced Rum Shrimp	136
Tequila Sunrise Snapper	138
Desert Chili Shrimp	140
Southwest Seasoned Fish Fry	142
Gringo Ginger Shrimp	144
Southwest Scented Tilapia	146
Stir Fry Mesa Shrimp	148

Salads

Baja BLT Salad	150
Cornbread Salad with Homemade Ranch Dressing	152
Mexican Sweet Corn Salad	154
Bacon Cheddar Salad	156
Santa Fe Carrot Salad	157
Sautéed Prawn and Portobello Salad	158
Seared Steak Salad	160
Southwest Black-and-Blue Salad	162
Sweet Potato Salad	164
Whiskey Grilled Portobello Salad	166
Whiskey Cherry Salad	168

Side Dishes

Chilled Cherry Soup	169
Chilled Sherry and Avocado Soup	170
Casa Chili Soup	172
Sherry Sprouts	174
Spiced Latin Hushpuppies	176
Kahlúa Creamed Corn	178
Mexican Medallions of Corn	179
Picante Potatoes	180
San Antonio Sautéed Mushrooms	182
Yellow Split Pea Soup	184

Baja Flank Ribs with Tequila and Honey Glaze

(Serves 4)

Flank ribs are one of the most popular ribs here in the Southwest. If you have never heard of this type of beef ribs, you are in for a real treat, and they are usually available at all markets and rather inexpensive. They are thinly cut slabs of ribs with their bone intact. They are only about a half-inch thick and each slab has about eight to ten little ribs on them (some regions call them riblettes). Usually you can figure on two slabs per person for a main course. Due to the fact that they are so thin, they cook up in only a matter of minutes.

Flank ribs are the perfect rib to marinate; due to their thinness, they become fully flavored in about thirty minutes. The marinade we use for this dish is a seasoned tequila marinade, and the flavors go perfectly with these ribs. Then what we do is glaze them, and there is even more tequila involved. The glaze is a tangy and slightly sweet sauce made with tequila, honey, and lime juice. These can either be prepared outside on a grill or inside using a grill pan (or under the broiler).

Due to the fact that you are going to be using tequila, you do want to be very careful. Any type of alcohol, when used in conjunction with a flame or intense heat, can cause a flame-up. In this case, the tequila will be diluted with other ingredients, but you still want to be very careful and always practice caution.

Ingredients
8 slabs beef flank ribs
1 tsp. garlic powder
1 tsp. ground cumin
1 tsp. chili powder
1 tsp. salt
¼ cup tequila
1 lime, juice and finely grated zest
1 Tbs. Chili Oil (page 29)
vegetable oil

For Tequila Honey Glaze
1 Tbs. raw honey
½ lime, juice only
¼ cup tequila

Steps

1. Keep the ribs on their slabs (don't cut them) and place them in a shallow non-aluminum dish.

2. In a small bowl, whisk the garlic powder, cumin, chili powder, salt, tequila, lime juice, lime zest, and Chili Oil.

3. Pour the marinade over the flank ribs and toss them to coat with the marinade.

4. Let the flank ribs marinate 30 minutes at room temperature.

5. Heat a grill or grill pan. If using a grill, brush the grill with some vegetable oil. If using a grill pan, add a tablespoon of vegetable oil.

6. Place the ribs on the grill (or pan) and cook about 5 minutes per side (less time if they are very thin).

7. Next, prepare the Tequila Honey Glaze. In a small pan over medium heat, whisk the honey and lime juice for 3 minutes.

8. Remove the pan from the heat and whisk in the tequila.

9. Place the pan back on the heat and cook 2 minutes.

10. Remove the flank ribs and place onto a serving platter.

11. Spoon the Tequila Honey Glaze over the ribs and serve.

Whiskey Maple Glazed Ribs

(Serves 4)

If you were to compare the smaller Baja Flank Ribs (page 64) side-by-side with these Whiskey Maple Glazed Ribs, you would think you are Fred Flintstone eating one of his brontosaurus ribs!

First of all, you are going to need an entire slab of ribs for this dish. In most cases, a typical supermarket will not sell a whole slab, but you can find them at restaurant supply stores, which are usually open to the public. You can also buy a few packages of beef ribs at your local market to make a whole slab. A whole slab of ribs will feed four people (remember you'll have other dishes at the table). As far as what type of beef rib, that option is yours as this recipe will work with any beef rib (and pork ribs as well).

Should you or shouldn't you trim the fat from your ribs? Here in the Southwest, we do not trim the fat off our ribs until after they have been cooked, and the reason is rather simple: the fat will protect the meat from the intense heat. The fat will also keep the meat moist during the cooking process. Remember, fat is flavor. Once the meat has been cooked, you can remove and discard the fat if you like.

Ingredients

1 slab beef ribs, untrimmed
½ cup whiskey (or bourbon)
1 Tbs. garlic salt
1 Tbs. garlic powder
1 tsp. ground black pepper
1 Tbs. Worcestershire sauce
1 cup Whiskey and Maple Glaze (page 8)

Steps

1. Dry the ribs to remove any moisture.
2. In a medium bowl, whisk the whiskey, garlic salt, garlic powder, black pepper, and Worcestershire sauce.
3. Place the ribs in a large shallow dish or roasting pan and pour the marinade over the ribs. Large zip-lock bags also work quite well.
4. Turn the ribs over a few times to coat them with the marinade.
5. Let the ribs marinate at room temperature for 1 hour.
6. Pre-heat your oven to 375°F.

7. Place the ribs on a large broiling pan or in a large roasting pan.

8. Place into the oven and cook 20 minutes per side (time may vary, depending on the amount of meat on the ribs or variety of the ribs).

9. Remove the ribs from the oven; at this time, you can remove any fat if you so choose.

10. Pre-heat your broiler.

11. Brush the ribs with some of the Whiskey Maple Glaze.

12. Place into the broiler for 5 minutes.

13. Turn the ribs over and brush them with some more glaze.

14. Broil for another 5 minutes.

15. Remove the ribs and let them rest 5 minutes.

16. Cut the ribs between the bones and serve.

Braised Short Ribs

(Serves 4)

In many areas of the United States, there seems to be some confusion regarding short ribs. Earlier in this section, I shared with you the recipe for Baja Flank Ribs with Tequila and Honey Glaze (page 64), and in that dish, I used flank ribs—which some people will call "short ribs" because . . . they're short! In some Asian eateries, they use this same type of ribs and call them "Korean short ribs." The fact of the matter is, a short rib is really nothing like a flank rib, other than that they are short, but they are also thick and quite meaty. In the butcher section of most supermarkets, you will find actual short ribs, like the ones called for in this dish.

The usual and best way to prepare short ribs is to braise them. Braising is simply a long cooking process in liquid. It is almost impossible to mess up a braised dish—almost because you do have to check the liquid content from time to time. Braising is best for short ribs because it breaks down the fibers in the meat, thus making it much more tender, and in the case of these short ribs, the meat almost literally falls off the bone.

The origin of this dish actually comes from the cowboys who roamed the great American Southwest. There have been some adaptations over time, but the taste and texture is the same as it was in those dusty days of yore. A big pan of braised short ribs is the quintessential Sunday Southwest dinner.

Ingredients

5 pounds beef short ribs (you want about 2 per person)

1 tsp. salt

½ tsp. ground black pepper

½ cup flour

2 Tbs. Cinnamon Oil (page 30)

2 white onions, peeled and thinly sliced

¾ cup Cinnamon Scented Ketchup (page 18)

¾ cup water

¼ cup brown sugar

¼ cup soy sauce

3 Tbs. Worcestershire sauce

2 Tbs. apple cider vinegar

¼ tsp. ground cayenne pepper

Steps

1. Using a paper towel, pat the short ribs dry of any moisture.
2. In a small bowl, whisk the salt, pepper, and flour.
3. Place the short ribs on a plate and dredge (coat) with the seasoned flour.
4. In large oven-safe sauté pan, heat the Cinnamon Oil over medium heat. Add the short ribs and brown on all sides.
5. Pre-heat your oven to 325°F.
6. Remove all the rendered fat from the sauté pan.
7. Into the pan, add the onions, Cinnamon Scented Ketchup, water, brown sugar, soy sauce, Worcestershire sauce, apple cider vinegar, and cayenne pepper and stir to combine.
8. Place a lid on the pan, put into the oven, and braise 2½ hours (depending on the size of the short ribs).
9. Remove the pan from the oven and let the short ribs rest in the pan 5 minutes.
10. Remove the short ribs to a serving platter, drape with the sauce, and serve.

Jalapeño Tequila Bombs

(Serves 4)

There was a time when I would serve Jalapeño Tequila Bombs as an appetizer, and people would go nuts over them. It was due to their popularity that I decided to make a main course with this dish by simply using larger jalapeño peppers. Peppers and a spicy ground meat are one of the great taste treats of a true Southwest kitchen.

When it comes to the ground meat to make this dish, you can choose any kind you like as long as it is of a spicy variety. My personal favorite is to use a spicy linguiça, and when using a sausage of this ilk, you always want to make sure to remove the casing. If the sausage is a kind that does not crumble when you remove the casing, simply dice it or put it into a food processor and give it a few whirls.

To fill the peppers is quite easy. Just slice them in half lengthwise. With a small paring knife, remove the seeds and membrane (white pithy stuff). If you want extra heat, leave some of the seeds. Using a small spoon, fill the open crevice of the pepper and make sure to mound it a little as the filling often shrinks while cooking.

Ingredients

12 large jalapeño peppers
1 Tbs. Cumin Oil (page 31)
½ white onion, peeled and minced
1 linguiça sausage, casing removed and sausage minced
1 cup shredded cheddar cheese
½ cup white tequila
¼ cup water

Steps

1. Slice the peppers in half lengthwise. Remove the seeds and membrane (white pithy part) and set aside.

2. In a medium sauté pan, heat the Cumin Oil over medium heat. Add the onion and sauté 5 minutes.

3. Add the linguiça and sauté 5 minutes.

4. Remove the pan from the heat and stir in the cheese until the mixture comes together.

5. Fill the peppers with the sausage mixture, slightly mounding the middle.

6. Clean out the sauté pan and then place over medium heat.

7. Stir in the tequila and water and bring to a simmer.

8. Add the peppers, cover the pan, and cook 5 minutes.

9. Remove the peppers to a serving plate, drizzle with some of the tequila cooking liquid, and serve.

Kahlúa Country Style Pork Ribs

(Serves 4)

Though we do love our beef ribs here in the Southwest, the favorite type of rib is still probably pork ribs, and when it comes to pork ribs, there are some outstanding cuts. One of the meatiest may be what is often referred to as "country style pork ribs." These are meaty slabs of pork consisting of two or three sections. You can find them at any supermarket, and they are usually quite inexpensive as far as ribs are concerned. Since these "ribs" have more meat than bone on them, they do take a little longer to cook.

Whoever it was that first decided to pair Kahlúa with pork should win some sort of Nobel Prize for food. There is just something about the sweet coffee flavor of this alcoholic beverage and the taste of a good piece of pork which was meant for each other. One of the great things about grilling or broiling with a high-sugar liqueur such as Kahlúa is the fact that the sugars in it will caramelize with the intense heat, adding even more flavor.

There are two ways you can prepare Kahlúa Country Style Pork Ribs. They can be grilled (perfect for a Southwest summer night), or they can be broiled (perfect for a Southwest winter night). Because the dish does contain Kahlúa, which has a small percentage of alcohol, you do want to watch for flame-ups. If you are grilling and you get a flame-up, just move the ribs to another part of the grill until the flame subsides. If using a broiler, you want the rack under the broiler to be one or two notches down from the heat source.

Ingredients

½ cup Kahlúa
1 Tbs. brown sugar
½ tsp. salt
½ tsp. ground black pepper
1 tsp. garlic powder
4 slabs country style pork ribs

Steps

1. In a small bowl, whisk the Kahlúa, brown sugar, salt, pepper, and garlic powder.
2. Place the ribs into a shallow bowl.
3. Pour the marinade over the ribs and turn them a few times to coat them.
4. Let the ribs marinate at room temperature for 1 hour.
5. Pre-heat your broiler or grill. If using a grill, brush it with some vegetable oil. If using a broiling pan, there is no need for oil.

6. Place the ribs on the grill or in the broiler and cook to desired doneness (at least 150–160°F on a meat thermometer). Give them a few brushes of the marinade (on each side) while they are cooking.

7. Remove from the grill or broiler and let rest 5 minutes before serving.

··· Note ···

Many times you will find pork country style ribs which are boneless. If this is the case, I usually like to slice them before presenting them at the table.

Kahlúa Glazed Flank Ribs

(Serves 4)

In the recipe for Baja Flank Ribs with Tequila and Honey Glaze (page 64), I talked about beef flank ribs, and we went into some detail on these tasty little ribs. If you tried that recipe and enjoyed the ribs, you are simply going to go gaga (no offense to the Lady with that last name) over these tasty little gems.

What we are going to do with these particular beef flank ribs is a very simple grilling. Then we are going to make a very simple Kahlúa glaze. How simple is the glaze? The only ingredient is Kahlúa—it can't get any simpler than that. We are going to take the Kahlúa and cook it down (reduce the liquid in it). What you are going to end up with is like a Kahlúa syrup (on a side note, you can use this very same syrup over vanilla ice cream—YUM).

This dish does contain a very popular spice we happen to love here in the Southwest, and it is called cumin. You can buy ground cumin at all supermarkets, but for the ultimate in taste, you will want to grind your own. Just buy some cumin seeds, place them into a coffee or spice grinder, and grind them until they are a powder. The taste difference between freshly ground spices and store-bought is night and day (and it saves you a lot of money in the long run).

Ingredients

8 slabs beef flank ribs (2 slabs per person)
1 tsp. salt
½ tsp. ground black pepper
1 tsp. garlic powder
1 tsp. ground cumin
½ cup Kahlúa

Steps

1. Wipe the beef flank ribs of any excess moisture.
2. In a small bowl, whisk the salt, black pepper, garlic powder, and cumin.
3. Place the flank ribs on a plate and season them on both sides with the spice mixture.
4. Let the ribs rest at room temperature for 30 minutes.
5. Pre-heat a grill or grilling pan and brush with vegetable oil.
6. Place the ribs on the grill or grilling pan and cook 5 minutes per side.

7. In a small pot over medium heat, add the Kahlúa and bring to a boil.
8. Reduce the heat under the Kahlúa to a simmer and cook 2 minutes.
9. Remove the ribs from the grill or grilling pan and place on a serving platter.
10. Spoon the Kahlúa over the ribs and serve.

Poached Poblano Peppers

(Serves 4)

To be totally honest, we do indeed love our poblano peppers here in the Southwest. A poblano pepper is the big cousin of the jalapeño pepper. They have about the same amount of heat (not too much) and are the chili pepper that is most often used to make the famous Mexican dish called chili rellenos. Fun fact: When poblano peppers are dried, they not only take on a different look, they take on a different name; a dried poblano pepper is an ancho pepper!

When you venture into a garden in the Southwest, you will usually see a few different varieties of peppers growing, and one of them will always be the poblano pepper. It is for this reason they are so popular in our kitchens. This dish, Poached Poblano Peppers, is almost like a Southwest version of chili rellenos—almost, simply because it has a meat stuffing. Poblano peppers are great for dishes such as this due to their skin being rather resilient against ripping during the cooking process.

We are going to fill these peppers differently than we would the Jalapeño Tequila Bombs (page 70). To fill these, you will need a pastry bag and a plain round tip. Once you have the bag filled, just place the tip into the reamed-out pepper and squeeze the filling in. You do want to overfill it slightly as the filling will shrink (lose some moisture) as it is being poached. This is really a simple procedure and pretty hard to mess up.

Ingredients

1 pound chorizo sausage, casing removed
4 cloves garlic, peeled and minced
4 dates, pitted and chopped
1 tsp. ground cumin
2 Tbs. yellow cornmeal
2 cups grated Monterey Jack cheese
8 large poblano peppers
1 cup tequila
½ cup grenadine

Steps

1. Heat a large sauté pan over medium heat. Add the chorizo and cook 5 minutes.

2. Stir in the garlic, dates, cumin, cornmeal, and cheese and cook 5 minutes.

3. Remove the pan from the heat and let cool.

4. Remove the stem end of the poblano peppers and discard them. Using a sharp paring knife, ream the inside of the peppers (removing the seeds and membranes).

5. Place the chorizo filling into a piping bag fitted with a large plain tip.

6. Place the tip of the piping bag into the pepper and fill each one.

7. Set the peppers aside and let rest for 10 minutes.

8. Into the same pan the chorizo was cooked in, stir in the tequila and grenadine over medium heat until it comes to a simmer.

9. Place the filled peppers into the pan, cover, and cook 7 minutes (depending on the size of the peppers).

10. With a slotted spoon, remove the filled peppers to a serving platter.

11. Spoon some of the sauce over the peppers and serve.

··· Note ···

If you have never used chorizo sausage before, it is different than most others. Once you remove the sausage from its casing and begin to cook it, it will almost liquefy. This is normal; you haven't done anything wrong!

Port Braised Short Ribs

(Serves 4)

If you were to trace this dish back to its origins, you would end up somewhere in Spain, and instead of a port wine being used for the braising liquid, it would be one of the famed Spanish sherries. About a century ago, give or take a decade, the grapes used to make port wine became a popular crop in parts of the Southwest, and when one has wine, one likes to use it in cooking.

There are many varieties of port wine on the market today, and they are usually quite reasonably priced. The type of port you are going to want for Port Braised Short Ribs is one of the sweet varieties, so do not buy any that say "dry" on their label. You can also use a "tawny port," or if you can't find a port wine (or if it is too expensive), use a sherry or marsala wine.

You may notice something rather interesting about the list of ingredients. We are not going to be using any onions. Most braised dishes, especially where beef is concerned, will include onions. In this case, with our braising liquid being a sweet wine, onions will interfere with the flavors and create an acid overload. Instead, we will be using green onions (or scallions or spring onions or whatever you want to call them—by the way, these are considered shoots of the onion bulb and not an onion per se).

Ingredients

5 pounds beef short ribs
1 tsp. salt
½ tsp. ground black pepper
¼ cup flour
2 Tbs. Basil Oil (page 28)
1 cup port wine
6 whole cloves garlic, peeled
2 green onions, chopped
1 Tbs. chili powder
1 cup water

Steps

1. Pre-heat your oven to 350°F.
2. Using a paper towel, wipe any excess moisture from the short ribs.
3. In a small bowl, whisk the salt, pepper, and flour.

4. Place the ribs into a shallow bowl and dredge (coat) with the seasoned flour.

5. In a large oven-safe sauté pan, heat the Basil Oil over medium heat. Add the short ribs and brown on all sides.

6. Remove any rendered (excess) fat from the pan.

7. Into the pan, add the port wine, garlic, green onions, chili powder, and water.

8. Place a lid on the pan, place into the oven, and braise 90 minutes.

9. Remove the lid and braise an additional 30 minutes.

10. Remove the short ribs from the oven and let rest in the sauce for 5 minutes.

11. Place the ribs on a serving platter, drape with the sauce, and serve.

··· Note ···

When braising (cooking in liquid), you always want to remember to check the liquid in the pan. If it is drying out (evaporating), add more port wine (or water).

Root Beer Ribs

(Serves 4)

Root beer and ribs? Yes, we are rather original here in the Southwest, but in reality, this is a great American dish. Let me explain. A long time ago, there was a very popular medicinal drink called sarsaparilla, and it was served in saloons all over the West. This drink was made from the smilax plant. It was sweet and sometimes used in cooking. This actual drink is no longer made in its original form; it has been bastardized into the soft drink we know today as root beer, and real root beer, the artisan variety, is indeed made from certain plant roots.

As you are very well aware, root beer is a carbonated beverage. Part of the reason it is carbonated is because it contains sodium (salt). Organic root beer also contains the previously mentioned plant roots and herbs. It is actually a perfect marinade. When you marinate the pork ribs, you do want the root beer to fizz up when you add it as this will help to tenderize the meat.

In some of the previous rib dishes in this section, I have noted that you shouldn't really remove the fat from the meat because the fat protects the meat from the intense heat and if you want to remove it, you should do so after the cooking. This is not the case with Root Beer Ribs. For this dish, you do want to trim the ribs of excess fat—but not all the fat. The reason is, you want the root beer to get into the fibers of the meat for the best possible flavor.

Ingredients

4 pound pork ribs (1 pound per person)
12-ounce bottle organic root beer
2 green onions, chopped
1 tsp. garlic powder
1 tsp. salt

Steps

1. With a paper towel, wipe any excess moisture from the pork ribs.

2. Place the ribs into a shallow bowl.

3. Pour the root beer over the ribs. Turn the ribs a few times to coat them with the root beer.

4. Once the root beer has stopped fizzing, stir in the green onions, garlic powder, and salt.

5. Let the pork ribs marinate at room temperature for 1 hour.

6. Pre-heat your grill or broiler. Brush the grill or broiling pan with some vegetable oil.

7. Place the ribs on the grill or broiling pan and cook to your desired doneness (150–160°F on a meat thermometer).

8. Remove the ribs and place onto a serving platter.

9. Cut the ribs between the bones and serve.

--- Note ---

This recipe is for ribs with bones in them. If using a country style pork rib (often boneless), you will want less per person. The proper cooking temperature, however, will not change.

Southwest Grilled Rum Ribs

(Serves 4)

This recipe is for country style pork ribs, but you can really use any type of rib you like. Oftentimes during the summer when I am having a big Southwest shindig, I will use a couple of slabs of baby back ribs. For a typical dinner, however, I think country style pork ribs work perfectly, and since they are very meaty and usually have no bones, you only really need one per serving.

WARNING: Before we go any further, I must tell you this can be a dangerous dish to prepare. We are going to be using rum, and it will not be diluted. Rum has a pretty high alcohol point, and alcohol and intense heat are not really the best of friends. If you are going to broil these ribs, place the rack near the bottom, as far as possible from the heat source. If you are going to be grilling them, use a long pair of tongs, and if the flame-up gets too intense (it will flame up), move the ribs to an area of the grill with indirect heat. If you want to be totally safe and will be using beef flank ribs, you can make these on a grill pan (I have never had a flame-up with this method).

To add some freshness to this dish, we will be using jalapeño peppers. Jalapeño peppers are not a hot pepper, as far as peppers are concerned. If, however, you don't want any heat but just the flavor of the pepper, simply remove the seeds and membrane from the pepper as this is where most of the heat is located.

Ingredients

4 portions of pork country style ribs, trimmed of excess fat
½ cup spiced rum
4 cloves garlic, minced
2 jalapeño peppers, seeded and minced
1 Tbs. chili powder
1 Tbs. Cumin Oil (page 31)

Steps

1. Use a paper towel to wipe the ribs of any excess moisture.

2. In a large shallow dish, whisk the rum, garlic, jalapeño peppers, chili powder, and Cumin Oil.

3. Place the ribs into the marinade and turn them a few times to coat them.

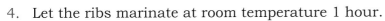

4. Let the ribs marinate at room temperature 1 hour.
5. Pre-heat your grill or broiler (see note above). Lightly oil the grill or broiling pan with vegetable oil.
6. Place the ribs on the grill or in the broiler and cook to desired doneness.
7. Remove the ribs to a serving platter and serve.

··· Note ···

If you want a glaze for these ribs (I usually do), pour the used marinade into a small saucepan and bring to a boil over medium heat. Keep cooking it until it has reduced by about half, and then before serving the ribs, brush them with the glaze.

Christmas Ribs

(Serves 4)

Spicy! Sweet! Colorful! Delicious! Those words don't just describe this wonderful pork rib dish, but they pretty much sum up the Christmas season in the Southwest. From what I have been able to determine, this dish was not created during a Christmas holiday. Apparently it gained its name because of it red hue, thanks to the use of grenadine. Regardless, I love to prepare these ribs for a Christmas dinner because they can surely warm the body and soul on a cold winter Southwest evening.

You can use any variety of pork ribs for this dish. I think it is outstanding with St. Louis–style ribs as they are a little meatier than other pork ribs, and the natural glaze created by the marinade adheres perfectly to the meat. I do not particularly like this with beef ribs as the meat on the beef ribs is not as naturally sweet as the pork.

Even though grenadine (which is a sweet syrup) is used in this recipe, the glaze on these ribs is not overly sweet since it is being tempered by the spiced rum. Also of note, there is not really enough rum in this recipe to cause any flame-ups, so if you want to grill these or broil closer to the heat, it should pose no problem.

Ingredients

4 pound pork ribs (1 pound per person)
2 tsp. Chili Oil (page 29)
1 tsp. ground cumin
1 tsp. garlic powder
1 tsp. garlic salt
1 tsp. chili powder
½ cup Cinnamon Oil (page 30)
2 Tbs. grenadine
2 Tbs. spiced rum

Steps

1. Using a paper towel, remove any excess moisture from the ribs.

2. In a large shallow dish, whisk the Chili Oil, cumin, garlic powder, garlic salt, chili powder, Cinnamon Oil, grenadine, and spiced rum.

3. Place the ribs into the marinade and turn over a few times to coat them with the marinade.

4. Let the ribs marinate 1 hour at room temperature.

5. Pre-heat your oven to 375°F.

6. Place the ribs into a roasting pan and roast 30 minutes, depending on the variety of ribs, or to desired doneness.

7. Pre-heat the broiler.

8. Brush the ribs with some of the marinade.

9. Place under the broiler and broil a few minutes per side.

10. Remove the ribs to serving platter and serve.

Southwest Bacon Burger

(Serves 4)

The simple fact is, you have never had a bacon burger unless you have had one the way we make them in the Southwest. As you will learn by the time you have finished trying out a few recipes from this book, we take our food very seriously, and that includes the simple burger. If you want a bacon burger, we will give you a bacon burger, and you will never forget it!

First of all, a bacon burger is not simply some lame patty of ground beef with a slice or two of bacon on it. We call that being lazy, unimaginative, and rather gross. That is the type of "thing" you would find in some fast-food place which should really be nowhere near your body. A bacon burger should be exactly what it is called: a bacon burger. It is really quite simple. You grind up the bacon and blend it into the ground beef. Not only does this give the burger an incredible flavor but the fat of the bacon will give you the moistest and juiciest hamburger you will ever have drip down your chin.

There is another secret to the great Southwest burgers. All the flavors get incorporated into the meat. We don't believe in messing up a burger with a bunch of stuff. You have everything incorporated into the meat, then you place it on a good quality bun, and simply kick back to enter burger nirvana (with an ice cold beer, of course).

Ingredients

½ pound smoked bacon
1 pound good quality ground beef
4 cloves garlic, minced
1 Tbs. chili powder
1 Tbs. Worcestershire sauce
1 Tbs. Red Chili Sauce (page 59)

Steps

1. Place the bacon into a food processor and process until finely chopped.
2. In a large bowl, combine the bacon, ground beef, garlic, chili powder, Worcestershire sauce, and Red Chili Sauce. Using your hands, combine everything very well.
3. Divide the mixture into 4 equal amounts and form into patties.
4. Let the patties rest 10 minutes.

5. Pre-heat a grill or griddle.
6. Place the patties on the grill or griddle and cook to desired doneness.

Barbecue Fried Chicken

(Serves 4)

We all have those days. Nothing seems to go as planned. Anything that can go wrong will go wrong. Then it comes time to make dinner, and we can't make up our minds. Do I want fried chicken? Do I want barbecued chicken? (No one ever said being an adult was easy) Here in the Southwest, we don't let this phase us—we do both. We make our famed Barbecue Fried Chicken!

If you're not from the Southwest, you are probably shaking your head in wonderment. This is actually one of the best fried chicken dishes you will ever taste. It is also one of the best barbecue chicken dishes you'll ever taste. Why? Because it is the best of both of these classic American dishes. And to answer the question you might be asking yourself, we are not actually going to take fried chicken outside and then barbecue it . . . but your family and friends will never know this.

This is an incredibly easy dish to prepare at home, and you really can't mess it up. You are simply going to fry a chicken. Once it is fried, you are going to submerge it in a barbecue sauce a few times and broil the sauce right into the chicken. Have a lot of napkins on hand, and be prepared for a literal symphony of lip-smacking.

Ingredients

1 whole chicken, cut into serving pieces
2 tsp. garlic powder
2 tsp. salt
1 tsp. ground black pepper
1 tsp. chili powder
1 tsp. dried tarragon, crumbled
½ cup flour
vegetable oil for frying
2 cups Cherry Barbecue Sauce (page 52)

Steps

1. Remove any excess fat from the chicken. Remember, skin is not fat!

2. In a large bowl, whisk the garlic powder, salt, pepper, chili powder, tarragon, and flour.

3. Place the chicken in the seasoned flour mixture and dredge (coat).

4. In a large sauté pan or skillet, heat 3 inches of oil to 325°F on a deep-fry thermometer.

5. Carefully place the chicken in the oil and fry 5 minutes per side.

6. Lower the heat to low, cover the pan, and cook the chicken 10 minutes per side.

7. Pre-heat the broiler.

8. Remove the chicken from the pan and place on a paper towel–lined plate to soak up any excess oil.

9. Place the barbecue sauce into a bowl.

10. Submerge the chicken pieces into the sauce; then place the chicken on a baking pan.

11. Place under the broiler and broil 3 minutes per side.

12. Remove the chicken and once again submerge into the barbecue sauce.

13. Place back under the broiler and broil 3 minutes per side.

14. Remove the chicken and let cool 5 minutes before serving.

··· Note ···

If you don't want to use a barbecue sauce for this dish and you want a little more spicy heat, use the Spicy Chipotle Glaze (page 12).

Bourbon Braised Turkey Necks

(Serves 4)

I know, you're looking at the title of this dish and shaking your head. No, we do not throw the turkey neck out when we prepare a turkey here in the Southwest. Matter of fact, we often head to the market and buy them by the pound. Why? Because turkey necks are quite delicious, and even better, they are very economical.

If you have never eaten a turkey neck, let me tell you the meat is very tender and quite rich. It is also fun to eat because you have to pick through all the little bones and tendons which make up the turkey neck. This is not really a main course you want to prepare for a black-tie dinner, but it is an outstanding dinner for family or friends to sit around and enjoy a great evening of food and frivolity.

You can find turkey necks at most markets year round. When you buy whole turkey necks, they are quite large, so you will want to cut them into pieces before you cook them. These turkey necks are going to be braised (cooked in liquid) which will tenderize them, and of course, the use of bourbon is also involved in the tenderizing process as well. When you do prepare this as a part of your dinner, be advised that, due to their richness, they are also quite filling.

Ingredients

2 pounds turkey necks
1 yellow onion, peeled and thinly sliced
1 Tbs. salt
1 tsp. ground black pepper
1 Tbs. garlic powder
2 Tbs. vegetable oil
1 cup bourbon (or whiskey)
½ cup water

Steps

1. Pre-heat your oven to 350°F.
2. Cut the turkey neck into 2-inch pieces.
3. Line the bottom of a roasting pan with the slices of onion.

4. In a small bowl, blend the salt, pepper, and garlic powder.
5. Rub the turkey necks with the vegetable oil and then season them with the salt mixture.
6. Place the turkey necks into the roasting pan.
7. Pour the bourbon and water over the turkey necks.
8. Place into the oven and roast 20 minutes per side.
9. Pre-heat your broiler.
10. Place the turkey necks into the broiler and broil a few minutes per side.
11. Remove the turkey necks from the broiler and let rest 5 minutes.
12. Place the turkey neck onto a platter and serve.

Chicken Española

(Serves 4)

As you go through the recipes in this section featuring chicken, you will probably notice that, here in the Southwest, we use mainly the dark meat of the bird, meaning the thighs and the legs. The reason for this is two-fold: First, they are the most flavorful parts of the chicken; secondly, they are the most inexpensive parts of the chicken. They are also the parts of the chicken which take the most time to cook, but as the adage goes, "good things come to those who wait."

One of the things I love about Chicken Española is that this dish really shows what the flavors of the Southwest are all about without having any heat. Here we will experience the herbs of our great region of America along with a slight touch of sweetness (from the grenadine) and a little kick from the blue agave (also known as tequila). This dish does have two different cooking times, as the chicken will first be cooked in a pan and then, to crisp up the skin, it will be placed under the broiler. Nothing difficult—and you can sip some sangria while you're doing it.

When it comes to preparing chicken thighs for any dish, make sure to remove any excess fat (there is quite a bit of it on the thighs—much like with humans). It is important, however, to remember that there is a difference between the skin and fat. Leave the skin intact—unless there are large pieces of skin overlapping the meat, then that can be removed.

Ingredients

4 large chicken thighs
6 green onions, minced
5 cloves garlic, minced
¼ cup minced cilantro
1 tsp. salt
2 tsp. ground cumin
2 Tbs. dried oregano, crumbled
1 cup gold tequila
½ cup grenadine
2 Tbs. vegetable oil

Steps

1. Remove any excess fat from the chicken thighs.
2. Into a large bowl, whisk the green onions, garlic, cilantro, salt, cumin, oregano, tequila, and grenadine.
3. Place the chicken in the marinade and turn a few times to coat.
4. Let the chicken marinate 1 hour at room temperature.
5. In a large sauté pan, heat the oil over medium heat.
6. Place the chicken in the pan, skin-side down, and cook 4 minutes.
7. Turn the chicken over, add the marinade to the pan, cover, and cook 25 minutes or until it reaches 160°F on a meat thermometer.
8. Pre-heat your broiler.
9. Place the chicken onto a broiling pan and broil, skin-side up, 2 minutes to crisp the skin.
10. Remove the chicken from the broiler and let rest a few minutes.
11. Place the chicken on a serving platter and serve.

Chicken Merlot

(Serves 4)

The Southwest portion of the United States is rapidly becoming a wonderful wine-making area, and the amount of prize-winning wineries are making this land traditionally known for tequila to be quite a player in the world of fermented grapes. When it comes to cooking, wine is the most versatile of alcohol products, and it goes wonderfully with any type of meat—especially so with chicken in general, and the dark meat of the chicken in particular.

Chicken Merlot is exactly what its title suggests. It is chicken cooked in merlot. It is not a spicy dish at all, but it does feature some of the herbs which create the flavors of the great American Southwest. When it comes to cooking with herbs, dried herbs are really just as good as fresh herbs, but you do have to watch how you use them. The rule of thumb is to use half the amount of dried herbs as you would fresh herbs. Why? Dried herbs have a more condensed flavor. Usually recipes (as in this book) will tell you if the amount is for "dried" or "fresh."

And now a word about cooking with wine. Never cook with a so-called "cooking wine." First of all, these are abysmal products. Secondly, they are laden with salt. The only types of wine to cook with are the types you would drink.

Ingredients

8 chicken legs
1 tsp. salt
½ tsp. ground black pepper
2 Tbs. vegetable oil
1 yellow onion, peeled and chopped
6 cloves garlic, peeled and minced
1 cup Mexican Tomato Sauce (page 58)
2 cups merlot wine
1 tsp. dried marjoram, crumbled
1 tsp. dried thyme, crumbled
1 tsp. dried oregano

Steps

1. Remove the lower part of the leg bone (the part you grab).
2. Season the chicken legs with the salt and pepper.

3. In a large sauté pan, heat the vegetable oil over medium heat. Place the chicken legs into the pan and brown them.

4. Remove the chicken legs and set them aside.

5. Into the pan, add the onion and garlic and sauté 5 minutes.

6. Place the chicken back into the pan and add the Mexican Tomato Sauce, merlot, marjoram, thyme, and oregano and bring the mixture to a boil.

7. Reduce the heat to a simmer. Cover the pan and cook 40 minutes.

8. Remove the chicken legs to a serving platter.

9. Drape the sauce over the chicken and serve.

Chicken with Cherry Salsa

(Serves 4)

I often get asked, why is the dark meat of the chicken more flavorful than the white meat? The answer is quite simple. The dark meat of the little bird has more fat in it, and fat equates to flavor. It is also "chewier" since the legs and thighs (the dark meat) are more muscular, and the more we chew food, the tastier it can become. Here in the Southwest, we much prefer the dark meat to the white meat (breast meat) for these simple reasons.

This beautiful Chicken with Cherry Salsa is basically roasted chicken thighs, lightly herbed, and served with a cherry salsa. Simple enough. What isn't simple, however, is the incredible amount of flavor this dish packs. We created this cherry salsa specifically for this dish, and the slightly sweet and slightly piquant flavor is perfect with the slight herbed flavor of the chicken.

You will first want to make the cherry salsa, and you can do this a few days ahead of time. If cherries are not in season, there are some wonderful organic canned cherries on the market today, usually sold as "sour" cherries. They're not really sour and work well for making this salsa. If you do use those cherries, drain them from their liquid and give them a quick rinse under cold running water.

For Cherry Salsa

½ cup minced parsley
¼ cup minced shallots
2 jalapeño peppers, minced
1 lime, juice only
3 Tbs. olive oil
1 pound cherries, pitted and halved

For Chicken

½ cup minced parsley
¼ cup minced shallots
4 limes, juice only
½ cup olive oil
8 chicken thighs, trimmed of excess fat

Steps

1. Place all of the Cherry Salsa ingredients into a medium, non-aluminum bowl and toss to coat.
2. Cover the bowl with plastic wrap and chill until ready to use.
3. Into a large shallow bowl, whisk the parsley, shallots, lime juice, and olive oil.
4. Place the chicken thighs into the marinade and toss a few times to coat.
5. Let the chicken marinate 30 minutes at room temperature.
6. Pre-heat your oven to 350°F.

7. Place the chicken in a large oven-safe sauté pan.

8. Place the pan in the oven and roast 25 minutes per side or to desired doneness (at least 160°F on a meat thermometer).

9. Remove the chicken from the oven and place two thighs on each serving plate.

10. Top with the Cherry Salsa and serve.

Chicken Zinfandel

(Serves 4)

When you take a look at a recent map of the American Southwest, you will notice many great grape-growing regions. Southwest wines are really beginning to find mass popularity not just within the United States but across the world. One of the great wines made in the Southwest is the zinfandel, and due to the climate, our variety of zinfandel has a fresh blackberry, anise, and slight peppery fragrance to it. Of course when you serve this dish to friends and family, you also want to have a bottle or two of this wine on the table.

There is a rather famous Italian dish called chicken cacciatore. You have probably enjoyed this at one time or another. I guess you could say this is the Southwest version. It is a chicken braised (slow cooked in liquid) in wine. The chicken becomes so tender, it literally falls off the bone when you eat it. Quite a wonderful meal for those famed Southwest Sunday family dinners.

These types of dishes are becoming quite popular these days as the vegetable is cooked right along with the meat, thus this is really quite an elegant one-pot meal. Chicken Zinfandel is wonderful served over some grilled polenta or steamed rice. Simple and delicious—the hallmark of Southwest cuisine.

Ingredients

4 large chicken thighs
1 Tbs. Chili Oil (page 29)
1 Tbs. olive oil
1 Tbs. butter
1 yellow onion, peeled and thinly sliced
1 tsp. celery seeds
1 Tbs. marjoram, crumbled
2 cup zinfandel wine
2 cups sliced carrots

Steps

1. Remove any excess fat from the chicken thighs and discard.
2. In a large sauté pan or skillet, heat the Chili Oil, olive oil, and butter over medium heat until the butter melts.
3. Add the chicken and brown on both sides.

4. Add the onion, celery seeds, marjoram, and wine and bring to a boil.
5. Reduce the heat to a simmer, cover, and cook 30 minutes.
6. Add the carrots, cover, and cook 15 minutes.
7. Remove the chicken to a serving platter.
8. Spoon the carrots around the chicken, spoon the sauce atop, and serve.

Frisco Funky Fried Chicken

(Serves 4)

When it comes to the art of fried chicken, there are two places in America which cannot be beat. There is the South, and there is the Southwest. Naturally, we believe ours is better, and we know it is more original. The main difference is that, many times in the South, the chicken will be battered before it is fried, whereas in the Southwest, we usually dredge (coat) the chicken in a spiced mixture and then fry it. With Frisco Funky Fried Chicken, we do let it soak for a bit.

Soaking chicken in a vinegar mixture (or buttermilk as they do in the South) creates a natural tenderizing solution. In the case of Frisco Funky Fried Chicken, we are going to be using a raspberry vinegar (slightly sweet), and instead of mixing it with milk, we will be using heavy cream. This will add some richness to the chicken. Now, you might be wondering, won't the vinegar curdle the cream? Yes, it will, and this is what we want.

Frisco Funky Fried Chicken is usually made with chicken legs (as we present it here), but you can make it with whatever part of the chicken you like the best. If, however, you are going to use the white meat section of the chicken (breast meat), your cooking times will be reduced.

Ingredients

8 chicken legs
½ cup heavy cream
2 Tbs. raspberry vinegar
½ cup flour
1 Tbs. garlic powder
1 Tbs. ground cumin
1 Tbs. salt
1 Tbs. ground black pepper
vegetable oil for frying

Steps

1. Place the chicken legs into a large shallow dish.

2. In a medium bowl, whisk the heavy cream and raspberry vinegar.

3. Pour the mixture over the chicken legs and let them soak for 30 minutes at room temperature.

4. In a medium bowl, whisk the flour, garlic powder, cumin, salt, and pepper.

5. Remove the chicken from the cream mixture and dredge (coat) them with the seasoned flour.

6. Let the chicken sit 10 minutes.

7. In a large sauté pan or skillet, heat 2 inches of oil to 325°F on a deep-fry thermometer.

8. Carefully place the chicken into the oil and fry about 5 minutes per side (time may vary, depending on the size of the legs).

9. Reduce the heat to low, cover the pan, and cook the chicken 7 minutes per side (time may vary, depending on the size of the legs).

10. Remove the chicken to a paper towel–lined plate to collect any excess oil.

11. Place the chicken on a serving platter and serve.

Honey Stung Fried Chicken

(Serves 4)

The first time I ever had Honey Stung Fried Chicken was about thirty years ago, and ever since then, it has been one of my favorite ways to prepare fried chicken. By the way, when I first had this at a little café in New Mexico, it was called "Bee Vomit Chicken." Lovely, appetizing name, don't you think? I guess you can say they were being honest since honey is indeed bee vomit!

This is really two Southwest favorites wrapped into one recipe. Here, the fried chicken is prepared as it typically is made in the Southwest, meaning the spice blend is used in the seasoned flour. It is not spicy hot but the combination of garlic, cumin, and chili powder is a wonderful marriage of flavors. This is also a nice little mixture if you ever want to flour some pork chops before frying them.

It is best to make this dish featuring chicken legs and thighs as both have the same cooking time. If you were to include the wings and breasts, you'd have to remove them at a different time and keep a watch during the cooking process. Make sure you clean the thighs of any excess fat as chicken fat is pretty disgusting.

Ingredients
½ cup flour
1 Tbs. chili powder
1 Tbs. garlic powder
1 Tbs. ground cumin
1 Tbs. garlic salt
2 tsp. ground black pepper
8 chicken legs or thighs (or combination of the two)
vegetable oil for frying
raw honey for drizzling

Steps
1. In a medium bowl, whisk the flour, chili powder, garlic powder, ground cumin, garlic salt, and black pepper.

2. Place the chicken into the seasoned flour and dredge (coat).

3. Let the chicken rest while the oil is heating.

4. In a large sauté pan or skillet, heat 2-inches of oil to 325°F on a deep-fry thermometer.

5. Carefully place the chicken in the oil and fry 5 minutes per side.

6. Lower the heat to low, cover, and cook 10 minutes per side.

7. Remove the chicken to a paper towel–lined plate to soak up any excess oil.

8. Drizzle the chicken with raw honey and serve.

Kahlúa Braised Chicken

(Serves 4)

Oh look, a dish featuring Kahlúa. How strange is that? (He writes with absolute sarcasm.) Whereas tequila is the favorite liquor in the Southwest, Kahlúa is the favorite liqueur, and of course, it helps that both have a tasty history here. So, you might be wondering, what exactly is Kahlúa? It is a concoction of rum, corn syrup, coffee, and vanilla, and it does contain caffeine as actual coffee beans from Mexico are used to make Kahlúa. Kahlúa was first created in Mexico in 1936, and its name means "House of the Acolhua people" in the Veracruz language.

This is really quite a delicious way to prepare chicken as it will be braised in the Kahlúa, and to add a slight salty and smoky flavor, we will be adding some bacon as well. These two flavor combinations blend wonderfully with the spices and herbs which complete this dish. I usually only use chicken thighs to make this dish, but you can use legs—and if you're having a party, load the pan with chicken wings (though your cooking time will be different for wings).

When it comes to bacon, I highly recommend using bacon from your butcher. The bacon that comes in those plastic packages are loaded with preservatives and chemicals (the "juice" you see in the pack), and that stuff is just plain nasty. If you have a smoker, try making your own bacon—it is worth both the time and the effort.

Ingredients

4 large chicken thighs
¼ cup vegetable oil
1 sweet onion, peeled and thinly sliced
4 jalapeño peppers, seeded and sliced
1 tsp. chili powder
1 tsp. ground cumin
8 slices smoked bacon, chopped
½ cup Kahlúa

Steps

1. Remove any excess fat from the chicken and discard.
2. Pre-heat your oven to 375°F.
3. In a medium sauté pan, heat the oil over medium heat.
4. Add the chicken and brown on both sides.

5. Remove the chicken from the pan and set aside.
6. Into the pan, add the onion, jalapeño peppers, chili powder, and cumin and cook 3 minutes.
7. Stir in the bacon and Kahlúa and cook 2 minutes.
8. Place the chicken back into the pan.
9. Place into the oven and cook 35 minutes.
10. Remove the chicken to a serving platter.
11. Drape the chicken with the braising sauce and serve.

Punk'd Chicken

(Serves 4)

If you have ever been to one of the fast-food places that feature chicken on their menu, you have no doubt tried or seen something called "chicken fingers" or "chicken strips." The unfortunate fact of the matter is, these so-called chicken dishes contain a lot more than just chicken meat. Their main components are parts of the chicken you and I would throw away after cleaning the bird. Kind of gross, but such is the way of the fast-food industry. This is our version of these chicken dishes, and as you can see, they are one hundred percent pure chicken meat.

I came up with the method for making Punk'd Chicken during a party. We thought it would be a good idea to have a platter or two of spicy chicken strips on the table with a variety of dipping sauces. As is the normal way of doing things in the Southwest, I had to be different, so instead of the usual breast meat, I decided to use my favorite part of the bird: the thigh. To make this, you will need skinless and boneless thigh meat. You can buy it this way at your market, or you can skin and bone it yourself (it is very easy). If you do it yourself, you'll not only save money but also have some ingredients for homemade chicken stock!

You will want to cut the thigh meat into thin strips as this is a dish which would be considered a finger food. It is a fun party dish, either as an appetizer or an entrée; have various dipping sauces or salsas available on the table. Any of the sauces or salsas in the Southwest Pantry section will work wonderfully well.

Ingredients

6 chicken thighs, skinless, boneless, and cut into strips
½ cup buttermilk
1 Tbs. Red Chili Sauce (page 59)
½ cup flour
2 Tbs. garlic powder
1 Tbs. garlic salt
2 Tbs. chili powder
vegetable oil for frying

Steps

1. Place the chicken strips into a large bowl.
2. In a small bowl, whisk the buttermilk and Red Chili Sauce. Pour over the chicken, toss to coat, and let sit 30 minutes at room temperature.

3. In a medium bowl, whisk the flour, garlic powder, garlic salt, and chili powder.

4. Dredge (coat) the chicken in the seasoned flour.

5. In a large sauté pan or skillet, heat 2 inches of oil to 325°F on a deep-fry thermometer.

6. Carefully place the chicken in the oil (in batches if necessary) and fry until golden brown and at least 160°F on a meat thermometer.

7. Using a slotted spoon, remove the chicken and place on a paper towel–lined plate to drain of excess oil.

8. Serve the Punk'd Chicken with various dipping sauces.

Santa Fe Chicken Wings

(Serves 4)

Chicken wings! Who doesn't love gnawing on these tasty little tidbits of very-little-meat-but-tons-of-flavor? Before the entire nation became enamored with chicken wings and you could buy them at your local market for next to nothing, we here in the Southwest were enjoying these on a daily basis. Long before there was a fiasco known as buffalo wings, there were Santa Fe Chicken Wings!

You might have noticed something strange lately at the supermarket when you buy chicken wings. They are not the same chicken wings they once were. Whereas in years gone by, you would get the whole chicken wing, they now cut them differently. I almost feel like I am getting ripped off. And then they have these strange creatures called "wingettes," which are only one section of the wing. I really wish people would not mess with Mother Nature. We wing fans want wings and not something that doesn't even resemble wings!

Santa Fe Chicken Wings are the ultimate in a savory wing. Just look at that list of ingredients, and you can almost taste the vibrancy of the great American Southwest. These are not a spicy hot wing, but if that is your preference, once these are done cooking and while they are still hot, douse them with some chipotle sauce and then dig in!

Ingredients

1 cup buttermilk
2 Tbs. Roasted Garlic Sauce (page 61)
4 pounds chicken wings
1½ cups flour
¼ cup garlic powder
2 Tbs. ground cumin
2 Tbs. salt
¼ cup chili powder
vegetable oil for frying

Steps

1. In a large bowl, whisk the buttermilk and Roasted Garlic Sauce.
2. Place the chicken in the bowl and toss the wings to coat them. Let the wings marinate 1 hour at room temperature.
3. In a medium bowl, whisk the flour, garlic powder, cumin, salt, and chili powder.

4. Remove the wings from the buttermilk mixture and dredge (coat) them in the seasoned flour.

5. In a large sauté pan or skillet, heat 2 inches of oil to 325°F on a deep-fry thermometer.

6. Carefully place the wings into the pan (in batches if necessary) and fry 3 minutes per side.

7. Reduce the heat to low, place a lid on the pan, and cook 7 minutes per side.

8. Remove the wings to a paper towel–lined plate to soak up any excess oil.

9. Place the wings on a serving platter and serve with various sauces.

Spiced Southwest Tequila Chicken

(Serves 4)

Like any cuisine that relies on fresh flavors and tremendous tastes, the foods of the Southwest are often marinated, and the marinating process is for two basic reasons: first, for robust flavor; secondly, the ingredients of the marinade usually involve one or more natural tenderizing elements. In the case of Spiced Southwest Tequila Chicken, the main tenderizer is the alcohol in the tequila.

When it comes to cooking with tequila, does it matter if you use white or gold? As far as the flavor is concerned, no, it does not. If you are using the tequila for a sauce, it could make a difference. If it is a white sauce, you would want to use the "white" (clear) tequila to keep the sauce its natural color. These rules, it should be noted, do not really count when it comes to drinking tequila, but then after a few drinks, you don't care anyway.

There is something about Spiced Southwest Tequila Chicken which always reminded me of a Southwest summer, so we only served it during that season at Casa de Cuisine. Then, one night, I realized it is also a perfect dish to warm the body and spirit and would be a perfect main course for a winter menu. Now we serve it all the time. Tequila, chicken, and spices—life doesn't really get much better in the great American Southwest!

Ingredients

8 chicken legs
½ cup Chili Oil (page 29)
1 tsp. ground cumin
1 tsp. chili powder
1½ tsp. garlic powder
1 tsp. garlic salt
1 tsp. dried oregano, crumbled
¼ cup gold tequila

Steps

1. Remove the elongated bone from the chicken leg (the part you grab when you eat a drumstick).
2. Place the chicken into a large shallow bowl.

3. In a small bowl, whisk the Chili Oil, cumin, chili powder, garlic powder, garlic salt, oregano, and tequila.

4. Pour the marinade over the chicken and let marinate 30 minutes at room temperature.

5. Pre-heat your oven to 375°F.

6. Remove the chicken from the marinade and place into a medium oven-safe sauté pan. Spoon the marinade atop the chicken.

7. Place the chicken into the oven and cook 40 minutes or to at least 160°F on a meat thermometer.

8. Pre-heat your broiler.

9. Place the chicken under the broiler and broil until the skin gets crisp.

10. Remove the chicken from the broiler and let cool slightly before serving.

Skins and 'Shrooms

(Serves 4)

A few years ago there was a rage among some hoity-toity restaurants of serving fried chicken skins. Pretty much everyone who loves fried chicken also loves to munch on the seasoned crisp skin. Same thing with a perfectly roasted chicken. What's the first thing you go for? Right, the skin. Here in the Southwest we did find this rage rather amusing because we've been eating chicken skin for quite some time. The Southwest is known for its frugality—nothing goes to waste!

Now, you might be saying to yourself "but the skin is fatty!" No, the skin is not fatty. There is a difference between chicken fat and chicken skin. Chicken fat is around the joints of the bird and, in some areas, under the skin. When you are preparing chicken skin, you scrape the fat from under the skin. Another point regarding the preparation of chicken skin. You want to use fresh skin. If you use older chicken skin, it will not get crunchy and will almost be a little leathery. Where do you get chicken skin? Well, when you skin your own portions of chicken, save it and freeze it. You can also ask your butcher, and many times they will give it to you for free.

With Skins and 'Shrooms, we take chicken skins and go a little Southwest gourmet. We don't just plop portions of fried chicken skins on a plate. No, we sauté some lovely large portobello mushrooms, then we serve the skins in the portobello mushrooms, and top it all with a lovely, zesty onion glaze. This is truly a memorable dish!

Ingredients

¼ cup butter

4 large portobello mushrooms, stem end removed

8 large pieces of chicken skin (breast size)

¼ cup flour

1 tsp. chili powder

1 tsp. garlic powder

1 tsp. garlic salt

½ tsp. ground black pepper

1 Tbs. ground cumin

vegetable oil for frying

1 small white onion, peeled and thinly sliced

¼ cup Chili Oil (page 29)

¼ cup balsamic vinegar

Steps

1. In a large sauté pan, melt the butter over medium heat.

2. Add the mushrooms and sauté a few minutes on each side.

3. Remove the mushrooms from the pan and set aside.

4. Remove any fat from the chicken skins.

5. In a medium bowl, whisk the flour, chili powder, garlic powder, garlic salt, pepper, and cumin.

6. Place the chicken skins into the seasoned flour and dredge (coat) them.

7. In the sauté pan, heat 1 inch of oil to 350°F on a deep-fry thermometer.

8. Carefully add the chicken skins to the oil and fry until golden and crispy (it won't take long).

9. With a slotted spoon, remove the skins to a paper towel–lined plate to drain of excess oil. Then cut the skins to fit into the mushroom caps.

10. In a small sauté pan over medium heat, combine the white onion and Chili Oil and cook 5 minutes.

11. Stir in the balsamic vinegar and cook 5 minutes.

12. Into the caps of the portobello mushrooms, place (mound) the fried chicken skins.

13. Place the chicken skin–filled portobello mushrooms on a serving plate.

14. Spoon some of the onion glaze atop each mushroom and serve.

Spicy Kahlúa Chicken

(Serves 4)

Earlier in this section, for the recipe of Kahlúa Braised Chicken (page 104), I went into a little history of Kahlúa and what it is actually made from. It is interesting. Go back and read it. This dish is really unlike Kahlúa Braised Chicken, and it sort of brings the Asian elements of Southwest cooking to meet its natural Mexican and Latin American elements. It is also outstandingly delicious!

To prepare this dish, we are going to prepare our chicken thighs just as we did for Punk'd Chicken (page 106). You will want skinless and boneless chicken thighs. You can buy these at your local supermarket for a ridiculous price, or you can buy whole chicken thighs and bone and skin them yourself to save a lot of money (and have some chicken scraps to make homemade chicken stock).

When I prepare this at Casa de Cuisine, I make this dish in a wok. It is essentially a stir-fry dish, thus the Asian influence. You can, of course, make it in a sauté pan or skillet just as easily. When dealing with a liqueur such as Kahlúa, you don't really have to worry about any flame-up as the alcohol content is very low, but just to be on the safe side, when you add the Kahlúa, take the pan off the heat.

Ingredients

4 large chicken thighs, skinned and boned
2 Tbs. Chili Oil (page 29)
4 cloves garlic, peeled and minced
2 shallots, peeled and minced
1 tsp. Cumin Oil (page 31)
1 tsp. chili powder
¼ cup Kahlúa

Steps

1. Cut the chicken thigh meat into thin strips.
2. In a large sauté pan or skillet, heat the Chili Oil over medium heat.
3. Add the chicken and cook 5 minutes.
4. Add the garlic, shallots, Cumin Oil, and chili powder and cook 5 minutes.
5. Remove the pan from the heat and stir in the Kahlúa.
6. Place the pan back on the heat and cook 2 minutes.
7. Spoon over some steamed rice or grilled polenta and serve.

Paco Shrimp with Peppers

(Serves 4)

Peppers. The Southwest is known for its peppers. When most people think Southwest cuisine, they do in fact think peppers, mostly of the spicy hot varieties and of course our famous Hatch peppers. Though, there is another type of pepper we love and use often (as you will note from this cookbook), and that is the sweet pepper, or as it is better known, the bell pepper.

Paco Shrimp with Peppers is a wonderful fresh-tasting dish featuring the natural sweetness of peppers. The rule of thumb when it comes to sweet peppers is: the brighter the color, the sweeter the pepper. Here we will be using two of the sweetest peppers: red and yellow. Whenever I cook with sweet peppers, I like to peel them, and the reason is really twofold. First, the skin of peppers can be rather tough, and I think it takes away from the pleasure of eating them. Secondly, it makes the dish sweeter and gives the pepper a chance to color the finished dish. Peeling a pepper is easier if you cut the pepper into sections and use a serrated vegetable peeler (available at all kitchen stores).

When it comes to sweet peppers, you now have a choice of sizes in the supermarket. You will see little ones and the usual full-sized ones. With many peppers, the smaller ones would be more flavorful, but I don't really find this to be the case when it comes to sweet peppers (I do find it true when it comes to hot peppers). So when you are shopping for your sweet peppers to make this dish, go for whatever is less expensive.

Ingredients

1 pound medium shrimp, shells removed
¼ cup Chili Oil (page 29)
1 yellow sweet pepper, seeded and julienned (cut into long thin strips)
1 red sweet pepper, seeded and julienned (cut into long thin strips)
1 white onion, peeled and thinly sliced
2 tsp. chili powder

Steps

1. Rinse the shrimp under cold running water.
2. In a large sauté pan, heat the Chili Oil over medium heat.
3. Add both sweet peppers and onion and sauté 5 minutes.
4. Add the shrimp and chili powder and sauté an additional 5 minutes.
5. Serve over grilled polenta or with flour tortillas.

Baby Portobellos with Sautéed Shrimp

(Serves 4)

During your adventures into the produce section of your local supermarket, you have probably seen a plethora of mushrooms. Some may look familiar, and some may look strange. The large variety of mushrooms has led to the saying, "There is fungus among us," because that is exactly what mushrooms are—a fungus. It is interesting to note that no one really knows how many varieties of mushrooms there are in the world.

It is a pretty safe bet to say that stuffed mushrooms are one of the most popular dishes in the world, and every type of cuisine has their specialty, just as every cuisine has their favorite mushrooms. The secret to delicious stuffed mushrooms is what you stuff them with. You want the filling to compliment the mushroom in both taste and texture. What might be good in one mushroom will not necessarily be good in another mushroom. Here in the Southwest, we love to pair our mushrooms with seafood as both of their textures make for a wonderful experience for your mouth.

For Baby Portobellos with Sautéed Shrimp, we are going to use a small variety of shrimp called bay shrimp, or as some people know them, salad shrimp. They are tiny little things, only about as big as a section of your finger. They are quite delicious and oftentimes come already cooked, so you only need to heat them for a dish such as this. Bay shrimp can usually be found in the butcher section of your local supermarket, and they are quite inexpensive. If you must use a larger variety of shrimp, just chop them up before cooking them.

Ingredients

8 baby portobello mushrooms, stem end removed
½ pound bay shrimp (or any small variety of shrimp)
2 Tbs. Worcestershire sauce
2 Tbs. melted butter
2 Tbs. Lemon Oil (page 32)
2 shallots, peeled and minced
2 tsp. garlic powder
1 tsp. chili powder
¼ cup sherry

Steps

1. Wipe the mushrooms with a damp cloth to remove any dirt.

2. Rinse the bay shrimp under cold running water.

3. In a small bowl, whisk the Worcestershire sauce and melted butter.

4. In a medium bowl, whisk the Lemon Oil, shallots, garlic powder, chili powder, and sherry.

5. Add the bay shrimp to the Lemon Oil mixture and marinate 30 minutes at room temperature.

6. Pre-heat your broiler.

7. Heat a medium sauté pan or skillet over medium heat. Add the shrimp and marinade and cook 5 minutes.

8. Place the mushrooms on a baking sheet and brush with the butter mixture.

9. Place under the broiler for 2 minutes per side (or a little longer, depending on size of the mushrooms). Brush them with the Worcestershire-butter mixture when you turn them over.

10. Place the mushrooms on a serving platter.

11. Fill the mushrooms with the shrimp mixture and serve.

Broiled Salmon with Bourbon Glaze

(Serves 4)

When it comes to restaurants and seafood, the most ordered dish is salmon. There is just something about a perfectly prepared salmon fillet that people love. It may be the fresh taste. It may be the way it flakes onto your fork. It may be its beautiful color (when fresh). Whatever the reason may be, salmon rules the restaurant roost, and here in the Southwest, we treat it with the regality it deserves.

Broiling or grilling salmon is our choice for cooking this wonderful creature of the water, and here in the Southwest, we are lucky to get most of our salmon rather fresh. When either grilling or broiling salmon, I always recommend leaving the skin on and doing ninety percent of the cooking on the skin side. The reason for this is really quite simple. The skin of the salmon will protect the flesh from the intense heat, and as the heat goes through the skin, it will essentially steam the flesh. This will give you perfect salmon every time. Don't worry if the skin "burns" or "chars" because, once you remove it, you will find the flesh to be perfect.

A wonderful fish like salmon deserves the best glaze, and one of my favorite ways to prepare salmon is with this sweet Bourbon Glaze. We are going to combine bourbon (or whiskey) and honey with some herbs and then cook it down to a lovely glaze the color of amber. To say Broiled Salmon with Bourbon Glaze is delicious would be a gross understatement!

Ingredients

4 salmon fillets
2 Tbs. Cumin Oil (page 31)
1 Tbs. raspberry vinegar
salt and pepper to taste
¼ cup raw honey
½ cup bourbon (or whiskey)
1 shallot, peeled and minced
1 Tbs. capers, chopped
1 lemon, only the finely grated zest

> ··· Note ···
> The broiling time does depend on the thickness of the salmon and the doneness you personally prefer.

Steps

1. Using paper towels, pat the salmon dry.

2. In a small bowl, whisk the Cumin Oil and raspberry vinegar.

3. Place the salmon on a plate and season with salt and pepper.

4. Pour the vinegar marinade on the salmon and gently rub it in. Let the salmon rest 10 minutes at room temperature.

5. Pre-heat your broiler.

6. Place the salmon on a broiling pan, skin-side up (facing the heating implement), and broil 5 minutes.

7. In a small saucepan over medium heat, whisk the honey and bourbon and bring to a simmer.

8. Stir in the shallot, capers, and lemon zest. Bring to a boil and cook 5 minutes.

9. Remove the salmon skin and turn the fillets over. Place back under the broiler and broil 2 minutes.

10. Place the salmon on a serving platter.

11. Drape the glaze over the salmon fillets and serve.

Southwest Crab Cakes

(Serves 4)

Simply put, crab cakes are one of the great joys of being alive! You can make crab cakes with virtually any variety of crab; however, the best two to use are the blue crabs (East Coast) and the famed West Coast Dungeness crabs. Here in the Southwest, we really don't have much of a shoreline, so we get our crabs delivered from the Pacific Ocean, and we use the Dungeness crabs. If you do not have fresh (live) crabs where you are (or if they're too expensive), you can use some of the good quality canned crab found in the butcher section of many markets. Usually this will be labeled "lump" meat, meaning it is the meat from the body and not the claws. This will work fine for crab cakes. Do not buy the canned crab sold next to the cans of tuna on the shelf!

When it comes to crab cakes, people on the East Coast will say they have the best. People on the West Coast will say they have the best. I will prove to you with this recipe that the fact of the matter is, the Southwest has the best. What makes ours better? Spices, herbs, and a sauce to die for!

Crab cakes are not too big, but they are rather rich, so you can figure two crab cakes per person. That might not seem like much, but remember, this is part of a dinner, so other items of absolute yumminess will also be served. It is best to serve the crab cakes right after they come from the pan for the ultimate in taste and texture.

For Sauce

¼ cup Serrano Chili Mayonnaise (page 22)
2 Tbs. sour cream
1 tsp. Red Chili Sauce (page 59)
½ tsp. horseradish
½ tsp. salt
¼ tsp. ground black pepper

··· Note ···
The sauce can be made ahead of time.

For Crab Cakes

1 Dungeness crab (or equivalent of canned crab)
2 Tbs. Chipotle Mayonnaise (page 16)
1 tsp. Red Chili Sauce (page 59)
1 tsp. horseradish
4 green onions, chopped
2 cloves garlic, peeled and minced
1 jalapeño pepper, minced
2 Tbs. minced cilantro
2 eggs, beaten
2 cups fresh breadcrumbs (yes, you can use sourdough)
¼ cup Lemon Oil (page 32)

Steps

1. Into a medium bowl, whisk the Serrano Chili Mayonnaise, sour cream, Red Chili Sauce, horseradish, salt, and pepper until smooth. Cover the bowl with plastic wrap and chill until ready to use.

2. If using fresh crab, remove the meat from the shell. If using canned crab, drain the meat.

3. In a medium bowl, combine the Chipotle Mayonnaise, Red Chili Sauce, horseradish, green onions, garlic, jalapeño pepper, cilantro, eggs, and breadcrumbs until well combined.

4. Fold in the crab meat.

5. Divide the mixture into eight portions and pat into a cake.

6. Let the crab cakes rest 15 minutes.

7. In a large sauté pan or skillet, heat the Lemon Oil over medium heat.

8. Add the crab cakes and sauté 7 minutes.

9. Turn the crab cakes over and sauté 5 minutes.

10. Place the crab cakes onto a serving platter.

11. Spoon some of the sauce over the crab cakes and serve.

··· Note ···

Use ONLY fresh breadcrumbs. Dried breadcrumbs will turn these into little slabs of faux concrete. For fresh breadcrumbs, just pop some bread into a food processor and give it a few whirls.

Grilled Portobellos with Crab Anglaise

(Serves 4)

Usually in the Southwest, we are an earthy type of people when it comes to our food. We leave the fancy stuff to the Wall Street crowd and the aristocracy, but make no mistake about it, when we want to put on our uppity airs, we can present a gourmet dish like no other. We just add a Southwest flair to it, like with this Grilled Portobellos with Crab Anglaise.

As with our recipe for Southwest Crab Cakes (page 120), you can use either fresh crab or a good quality canned crab to make the Crab Anglaise for this dish. As for the portobello mushrooms, you can find them in the produce section of any supermarket. Just walk to the area where they have mushrooms, and you'll see them. They are huge, dark mushrooms, probably the biggest mushrooms on display. They do cost a little more than other mushrooms, but when you consider one mushroom will feed one person, it's not really too bad a deal.

The Crab Anglaise we are going to fill the mushrooms with is a French type of dish (with a definite Southwest flair), but don't let that scare you off. It is quite simple to make. It is quite rich and goes perfectly with the portobello mushrooms. This is truly a wonderful meal to make for any special occasion.

Ingredients

1 Dungeness crab
2 Tbs. Basil Oil (page 28)
1 Tbs. Worcestershire sauce
1 tsp. ground cumin
4 large portobello mushrooms, stem end removed
¼ cup butter
3 shallots, peeled and minced
4 cloves garlic, peeled and minced
4 jalapeño peppers, minced
8 slices bacon, minced
½ cup sour cream
3 Tbs. heavy cream

Steps

1. Remove the meat from the crab and discard the shells. If using canned crab, drain the meat.
2. Pre-heat your broiler.
3. In a small bowl, whisk the Basil Oil, Worcestershire sauce, and cumin.
4. Place the portobello mushrooms on a baking sheet and brush them (both sides) with the Basil Oil mixture.
5. Place the mushrooms under the broiler and broil 2–3 minutes per side (adjust time as needed, depending on their size).
6. Remove the mushrooms and set aside (keeping them on the pan).
7. In a medium sauté pan, melt the butter over medium heat.
8. Add the shallots, garlic, jalapeño peppers, and bacon and sauté 5 minutes.
9. Stir in the sour cream and heavy cream until it is blended.
10. Add the crab meat and cook 2 minutes.
11. Spoon some of the Crab Anglaise into the mushroom caps.
12. Place them back under the broiler and broil about 2 minutes (just until the Crab Anglaise starts to get a little color).
13. Remove from the broiler, let cool slightly, and serve.

Kahlúa Shrimp Azteca

(Serves 4)

Imagine, if you will, perfectly plump shrimp sautéed to perfection and covered with a sweet and spicy glaze. Well, imagine no more because that is exactly what Kahlúa Shrimp Azteca is! This is one of those dishes where you wish the plate will never empty. Sad to admit, but I have actually eaten a whole recipe of this by myself (and no, I have no regrets).

There are actually two ways you can cook Kahlúa Shrimp Azetca. You can cook it with the shells on the shrimp or with the shells removed. When you cook shrimp with their shells on, they are more flavorful, and the shells help protect the meat from intense heat. When you cook them with their shells off, they will shrink more, and you run the chance of easily overcooking them. If you cook them with their shells on, just have plenty of napkins at the table.

This dish can be a little spicy for some tongues. You can cut down on the spicy heat of Kahlúa Shrimp Azteca by removing the serranos' seeds and membrane (the white pithy stuff inside the pepper). If you want to increase the heat, you can use a chipotle chili powder instead of the usual red chili powder.

Ingredients

1 pound medium shrimp
½ cup Kahlúa
2 shallots, peeled and minced
2 serrano peppers, minced
2 tsp. chili powder
2 Tbs. Lemon Oil (page 32)

Steps

1. Rinse the shrimp under cold running water.
2. In a large bowl, whisk the Kahlúa, shallots, serrano peppers, and chili powder.
3. Place the shrimp in the bowl and marinate 30 minutes at room temperature.
4. In a large sauté pan or skillet, heat the Lemon Oil over medium heat.
5. Add the shrimp and sauté 5 minutes.

6. Add the marinade and cook 2 minutes.

7. Serve the Kahlúa Shrimp Azteca over some High Desert Cornbread (page 198) or some grilled polenta.

··· Note ···

Cooking time does vary, depending on the size of the shrimp being used.

Scallops in Mango Butter

(Serves 4)

Scallops have only become really popular in Southwest cuisine within the past decade or so. Though I don't know this for certain, I am sure a Southwest chef ventured towards the coast, brought some of these bivalves back, put them on his menu, and then when the locals tasted this gem of the ocean, they fell in love and wanted more. Yes, this is how food becomes popular.

There are two basic varieties of scallops (for eating). There is the sea scallop and the bay scallop. Both are from salt water. The sea scallop is quite large, and usually four are served per person for a main course. The bay scallops are small, about the size of a five-cent piece. We will be using the bay scallops for this dish, and you can find them at better markets with a fish/seafood section. You do want to make sure not to overcook scallops, or they can become rather tough.

The mango butter we are going to use for this dish is simply unreal. You will have the natural sweetness of the mango and the slight spiciness of the Southwest. This is a great butter (sauce) to serve with any shellfish and also quite wonderful with grilled chops, either lamb or pork.

Ingredients

1 pound bay scallops
¼ cup cornstarch
salt and pepper to taste
1 tsp. garlic powder
¼ cup butter
2 tsp. Chili Oil (page 29)
2 mangoes, peeled, pitted, and pureed

Steps

1. Using a paper towel, wipe the scallops of any excess moisture.
2. In a small bowl, whisk the cornstarch, salt, pepper, and garlic powder.
3. Dredge (coat) the scallops in the seasoned cornstarch.
4. In a large sauté pan, melt the butter over medium heat.
5. Add the scallops and sauté 5 minutes per side (depending on their size).
6. Remove the scallops to a plate and keep warm.
7. In the same sauté pan, heat the Chili Oil over medium heat.

8. Add the mango puree and stir 2 minutes.

9. Place the scallops onto serving plates.

10. Top each scallop with some mango butter and serve.

··· Note ···

I love serving this dish over freshly made pasta. You can also use a jasmine rice or creamy polenta.

Sherry Shrimp with Endive

(Serves 4)

As you may have surmised from most of the recipes in this book, we do love our gardens here in the Southwest, and we incorporate our bountiful harvests in many of our dishes. When pairing our foods with our garden goods, we think about how their flavors will mesh. In the case of Sherry Shrimp with Endive, this meshing of flavors is simply stunning.

Endive is an interesting vegetable. It is quite popular to grow in the Southwest because it can be grown in planters. You can also find it in many markets, but it can get to be a little confusing. Let me explain. What is known as endive in the United States is not really known as endive in other parts of the world. A perfect example of this is what is known as Belgian endive in the United States and known as chicory in many parts of Europe. For this recipe, when we say endive, we are in fact referring to the Belgian endive. Endive is a leafy vegetable with a slight bitter taste, which goes perfectly with the shrimp and sherry.

Of course the use of sherry, a sweet wine, is very popular within the Southwest, thanks to our Latin and Spanish influence. If you're not a fan of sherry or a good quality sherry is too expensive, you can always use a port wine or a Marsala wine, as long as neither are of the "dry" variety (meaning less sweet). You may notice something strange here. We are going to sauté the shells of the shrimp for this dish. Why? They have quite a bit of flavor and will naturally color the dish.

Ingredients

1 pound medium shrimp, peeled; set the shells aside
¼ cup butter
2 Tbs. olive oil
4 endive, julienned (cut into long thin strips)
2 green onions, minced
2 Roma tomatoes, chopped
1 cup sherry
1 lemon, juice and finely grated zest
½ cup grated Parmesan cheese

Steps

1. Rinse the shrimp under cold water and pat dry.

2. In a large sauté pan or skillet, melt the butter into the olive oil over medium heat.

3. Place the shells of the shrimp into the pan and sauté them for 3 minutes.
4. Remove the shrimp shells and discard them.
5. Add the shrimp to the pan and sauté 5 minutes.
6. Add the endive, green onion, and tomatoes and sauté 3 minutes.
7. Stir in the sherry, lemon juice, and lemon zest and cook 4 minutes.
8. Remove the pan from heat and sprinkle the Parmesan cheese atop.
9. Spoon onto plates and serve.

Shrimp de la Cancun

(Serves 4)

Why is Southwest cuisine one of the healthiest you can put into your body? Because our dishes always contain essential vitamins and minerals. We always include a good portion of produce. We tend to use low-fat cuts of meat and/or seafood. We are known for having fruit as a part of our main dishes. All of these pretty much sum up Shrimp de la Cancun—and then there is the added bonus of tequila!

You might have noticed that many dishes in Southwest cooking call for fresh lemon or lime juice. Before you juice the lemon or lime, make sure you zest it. I always zest all my citrus (even grapefruit), and I keep it in a zip-lock bag in the freezer. This way I always have zest on hand for those dishes which only call for zest.

Not all shrimp are created equal. You will notice in your fish market or butcher section a myriad of shrimp. Each one of these varieties cooks differently (timewise). When cooking shrimp, I use one basic rule for any of the varieties. Once they turn pink, they are essentially done. Why essentially? Because, even though you may remove them from the heat (or pan), they will still be cooking. So, whenever you see any recipe for shrimp (including in this book), remember this rule because I can't really know what type of shrimp you are using!

Ingredients

1 pound shrimp, peeled
1 Tbs. Chili Oil (page 29)
2 limes, juice only
1 tsp. ground cumin
1 tsp. chili powder
2 Tbs. Lemon Oil (page 32)
2 Tbs. butter
2 cloves garlic, peeled and minced
2 green onions, minced
1 mango, peeled, pitted, and chopped
1 cup gold tequila

Steps

1. Rinse the shrimp under cold running water and pat dry.
2. In a medium bowl, whisk the Chili Oil, lime juice, cumin, and chili powder.

3. Place the shrimp into the marinade and marinate 15 minutes at room temperature.

4. In a large sauté pan, heat the Lemon Oil and butter over medium heat and stir until the butter has melted.

5. Add the shrimp and sauté 5 minutes (time may vary, depending on size of shrimp).

6. Stir in the garlic and green onions and cook 1 minute.

7. Add the mango and sauté 2 minutes.

8. Remove the pan from the heat and stir in the tequila.

9. Serve over grilled polenta or wild rice.

Santa Ana Shrimp and Snapper

(Serves 4)

Red snapper has become one of the most popular eating fish within the United States, but there is a slight problem. Most red snapper sold is not really red snapper. The explanation here is long, but to put it in a nutshell, fish such as rockfish and sub-species of a fish called "snapper" are often sold as red snapper. For example, when you see "Pacific red snapper" at your market, it is not red snapper; it is usually a rockfish. The only real red snapper is northern red snapper and can be found in the Atlantic Ocean and the Gulf of Mexico. Confused? Don't be. Since you don't really have a choice in the matter (unless you personally catch it), just buy what they say is "red snapper."

If you have never had the experience of eating red snapper, you are in for one very special treat. It is a delicious white fleshy fish with a wonderful fresh flavor. If you have never cooked red snapper, don't worry. It is extremely versatile and is pretty hard to mess up. All supermarkets usually carry red snapper, and when it is on sale, it is quite inexpensive.

Santa Ana Shrimp and Snapper is a dish we created at Casa de Cuisine, and I must admit, it is one of my favorite ways to enjoy red snapper. You might notice a little something odd about this dish. We are going to combine two totally different types of seafood. Along with the red snapper, we will also be having small shrimp known as "baby" shrimp. Baby shrimp are available at all markets and sometimes sold under the name "salad shrimp." I truly hope you enjoy this dish as much as I did creating it.

Ingredients

4 red snapper fillets
1 tsp. dried thyme, crumbled
salt and pepper to taste
¼ cup Chili Oil (page 29)
2 Tbs. butter
4 shallots, peeled and minced
4 cloves garlic, peeled and minced
½ cup spiced rum
½ pound baby shrimp

Steps

1. Rinse the red snapper fillets under cold running water and pat dry.
2. Season the red snapper fillets with the thyme, salt, and pepper.
3. In a large sauté pan, heat the Chili Oil over medium heat and stir in the butter until it has melted.
4. Add the shallots and garlic and sauté 2 minutes.
5. Add the red snapper fillets and cook 5 minutes per side.
6. Remove the red snapper fillets to a serving platter.
7. With the pan off the heat, stir in the rum.
8. Place the pan back on the heat, add the baby shrimp, and cook 2 minutes.
9. Spoon baby shrimp over the red snapper fillets and serve.

Casa Red Snapper

(Serves 4)

There is an adage which goes, "Sometimes simple is the best." This is very true in a lot of aspects of life, and very often it is gospel in the kitchen, especially the Southwest kitchen. There is nothing wrong with something being simple. Matter of fact, most things in the kitchen are quite simple. It is our mind which makes us think they are difficult. This dish, Casa Red Snapper, is simple. I don't really think you can mess it up (unless you fall asleep when you put the fish on the grill).

In the recipe for Santa Ana Shrimp and Snapper (page 132), I went into some details of red snapper and why oftentimes what you may think is red snapper actually is not. Red snapper is available at most supermarkets, but if you don't like red snapper, you can actually make this dish with any fleshy type of fish, such as tilapia or catfish.

This makes for a great dinner during the hectic time of year (which for some people is every day) since it takes less than a half hour from start to finish. It is also quite economical as you probably already have most of the ingredients in your kitchen. Did I mention it was delicious and flavored with some rather healthy spices?

Ingredients

4 red snapper fillets
salt and pepper to taste
1 Tbs. Lemon Oil (page 32)
¼ cup butter
4 shallots, peeled and minced
2 tsp. Chili Oil (page 29)
2 tsp. ground cumin
2 tsp. chili powder
½ cup cooked bacon, chopped

Steps

1. Rinse the red snapper under cold running water and pat dry.

2. Season the red snapper fillets with salt and pepper.

3. Place a grill pan or large sauté pan over medium heat. If using a grill pan, brush with the Lemon Oil. If using a sauté pan, add the Lemon Oil while heating the pan.

4. Place the red snapper in the pan and grill or sauté 5 minutes per side.

5. Remove the red snapper from the pan and place on a serving platter.
6. In a small sauté pan, melt the butter over medium heat.
7. Add the shallots, chili oil, cumin, chili powder, and bacon and cook 5 minutes.
8. Spoon the sauce over the red snapper and serve.

Spiced Rum Shrimp

(Serves 4)

What we have here is very simple. We have rum. We have shrimp. Which means we have happiness. Okay, if that doesn't make you happy, we also have bacon! Rum, shrimp, and bacon is pretty much all this dish is. Almost makes you want to throw a party, doesn't it? And party food is exactly what this dish is!

First of all, let me tell you the classic way to present this dish to your friends or family if you want to be a true Southwesterner. Once you have prepared the Spiced Rum Shrimp, you fry up a bunch of onion rings (using Southwest sweet onions, of course). Once you have a nice pile of onion rings on the plate, you throw on some Spiced Rum Shrimp. Sometimes food can be fun and should be eaten with acute gaiety.

Regarding the rum, it will not be cooked or heated in any way, so you will be getting the full effect of the alcohol. Quite obviously, you will not want to serve this to anyone with an alcohol-related illness.

Ingredients
1 pound large shrimp, peeled
smoked bacon (see note for amount)
2 limes, thinly sliced
½ cup spiced rum

Steps
1. Rinse the shrimp under cold running water and pat dry.
2. Pre-heat your broiler.
3. Lay the slices of bacon out flat.
4. Place a shrimp at one end of the bacon and then wrap the bacon around the shrimp. Secure the ends with a toothpick.
5. Place the bacon wrapped shrimp on a baking sheet.
6. Place under the broiler and broil 5–7 minutes (until the bacon begins to get crisp).
7. Line the bottom of a serving platter with the slices of limes.
8. Remove the shrimp from the broiler and place upon the serving platter.
9. Spoon the rum over the shrimp and serve.

The Southwest Kitchen 🌶 137

Tequila Sunrise Snapper

(Serves 4)

One of the favorite adult beverages from the American Southwest is the famed Tequila Sunrise. One of the favorite fish served in Southwest eateries is red snapper. With this known, it only makes sense that one of the favorite dishes in the Southwest is Tequila Sunrise Snapper. Now, you might be thinking this is hyperbole. No, we really will be cooking red snapper in a Tequila Sunrise!

Tequila, grenadine, and orange juice are the ingredients to the classic Southwest drink called a Tequila Sunrise. Those very same ingredients are the basis for the sauce which will be lovingly draped over the red snapper fillets. We created this dish at Casa de Cuisine on a whim. I just thought that the fresh flavors of a Tequila Sunrise would enhance a dish featuring red snapper. I was right, and I think you will simply fall in love with this dish.

Now since this is the Southwest, we of course do have to add a few of our favorite spices and give this dish the famed Southwest kick. This is a very simple dish to prepare at home and rather quickly. By the way, we also prepare this very same dish with fresh trout—simply unreal!

Ingredients

4 red snapper fillets
1 tsp. ground cumin
1 tsp. chili powder
2 Tbs. butter
¼ cup Lemon Oil (page 32)
2 shallots, peeled and minced
½ cup tequila
¼ cup grenadine
3 Tbs. orange juice

Steps

1. Rinse the red snapper fillets under cold running water and pat dry.
2. Season each side of the red snapper fillets with the cumin and chili powder.
3. In a large sauté pan, melt the butter into the Lemon Oil over medium heat.
4. Add the red snapper fillets and sauté 5 minutes per side.
5. Remove the red snapper fillets to a serving platter and keep warm.

6. Into the sauté pan add the shallots and sauté 2 minutes.

7. In a medium bowl, whisk the tequila, grenadine, and orange juice.

8. Stir the tequila mixture into the sauté pan and bring to a boil.

9. Reduce the heat to a simmer and cook 5 minutes.

10. Spoon the sauce over the red snapper and serve.

Desert Chili Shrimp

(Serves 4)

If you pay attention to your surroundings when you go shopping at your favorite market, you will notice quite a few food products these days with the word "limon" on them. What is limon? The actual answer depends on what part of the world you are from. In most cases, the word "limon" simply means it has lime in it. It's worth noting that, in many Spanish-speaking regions, "limon" is used for both lemons and limes; however, some countries, like Peru, don't have any lemons at all, and the word is used exclusively for limes. The "limon"-lemon-lime debate is ongoing, but you can rest assured that, when you see "limon" on an otherwise English-labeled package, you're most likely looking at a lime-flavored product. Why don't they just use the word "lime" then? Because "limon" is a little more exotic, and the foods it is usually attached to are ethnic. Simply put, it is marketing.

With many of the products featuring "limon," you will also find spices, the most popular being chili powder. The reason for this is the simple fact that chili powder brings out the natural flavors of limes, and limes bring out the fresh flavor of the chili powder. It is for these two reasons that Desert Chili Shrimp is so good.

I think the only way to really prepare Desert Chili Shrimp is by using large shrimp, also known as prawns. If you really want to splurge, you can use the big freshwater prawns. This recipe calls for two pounds—this is if they are of the large variety. If you want to use the medium-sized variety, one pound will be sufficient for four people. If you really want to do the Southwest thing, you can even buy the whole shrimp, meaning with the heads on, but this does freak some people out.

Ingredients

2 pounds large shrimp (or 1 pound medium shrimp), shells left on
4 limes, juice only
2 Tbs. ground cumin
2 Tbs. chili powder
¼ cup Lemon Oil (page 32)
4 shallots, peeled and minced
4 cloves garlic, peeled and minced
1 tsp. salt

Steps

1. Rinse the shrimp under cold running water and pat dry.
2. In a large bowl, whisk the lime juice, cumin, and chili powder.

3. Place the shrimp into the marinade and marinate 30 minutes at room temperature.

4. In a large sauté pan, heat the Lemon Oil over medium heat.

5. Add the shallots, garlic, and salt and sauté 5 minutes.

6. Add the shrimp and marinade and sauté 7 minutes (time may vary, depending on the size of the shrimp).

7. Remove from the heat and let cool slightly before serving.

Southwest Seasoned Fish Fry

(Serves 4)

When it comes to the American tradition of the Friday Night Fish Fry, no one can beat the people of the Midwest. I don't think I have ever seen a food phenomenon take over an area like that before. All restaurants get involved. Even the Asian eateries would change their menu on Friday nights to have their version of a fish fry. It was fun trying everyone's "secret" batter for the fish (which always seemed to include beer).

Though a Friday Night Fish Fry in the Southwest is not as popular as in the Midwest, it is still practiced by many people, and we have our own type of batter for the fish. It doesn't include beer (nor tequila), but it does have a little spiciness to it. Whereas most places in the Midwest will fry their fish in huge vats of bubbling oil, we simply take out a sauté pan and do it in there. As far as what type of oil to use for this type of deep frying, I always prefer a peanut oil, but any type of vegetable or canola oil will work too.

Now to the fish. Fist fights have actually broken out over what fish should be used in a fish fry. Any type of fleshy fish will be able to withstand the heat without breaking up. I happen to be a fan of large pieces of white fish, but pollock or haddock will work well. Of course, if you spritz some malt vinegar on the fried fish (like I often do), it is fish-and-chips style!

Ingredients

2 cups flour
2 Tbs. baking powder
¼ cup cornstarch
1 tsp. baking soda
2 eggs, beaten
1½ cups ice water
1 tsp. salt
1 Tbs. garlic powder
2 Tbs. chili powder
8 large pieces white fish fillets
peanut oil for frying

Steps

1. In a large bowl, whisk the flour, baking powder, cornstarch, baking soda, eggs, ice water, salt, garlic powder, and chili powder until smooth.

2. Let the batter rest 20 minutes.

3. Rinse the fish fillets under cold running water and pat dry.

4. In a large sauté pan or deep skillet, heat 2 inches of oil to 350°F on a deep-fry thermometer.

5. Re-whisk the batter.

6. Dip each piece of fish in the batter to completely coat.

7. Carefully place into the oil (in batches if necessary) and fry until golden on both sides.

8. Remove the fish to a paper towel–lined plate to drain of any excess oil.

9. Let cool slightly before serving.

Gringo Ginger Shrimp

(Serves 4)

This particular dish, Gringo Ginger Shrimp, would be considered a "newer" dish in the realm of Southwest cuisine. As you will note from both the ingredients and preparation of the dish, it has Asian undertones. This is not unusual for Southwest cuisine when one considers that, when many of the states in the Southwest were just beginning, the Asian communities played a big role in their conception. It should also be noted that the word "gringo" is not racially charged nor a put-down and is actually used today in more of a humorous way.

For this dish, we are going to use a vegetable known as baby bok choy. If you are not used to Asian cuisine, bok choy is a form of Chinese cabbage, but have no fear, it doesn't taste anything like the cabbage most people are used to. You can find bok choy in the produce section of any supermarket. Baby bok choy is simply a smaller version of bok choy. It is quite delicious and considered one of nature's super foods.

This is not really a spicy dish at all (which is why it is called "gringo). It is, however, a very naturally flavorful dish. If you are worried about some heat due to the use of jalapeño peppers, simply remove the seeds and membrane (white pithy part of the inside of the peppers) before cooking them. The best type of shrimp to use for this dish is the medium variety.

Ingredients

1 pound shrimp, shelled
2 Tbs. Basil Oil (page 28)
2 Tbs. grated ginger
2 Tbs. Chili Oil (page 29)
4 scallions, minced
2 jalapeño peppers, julienned (cut into long thin strips)
4 baby bok choy, bases of each stalk removed

Steps

1. Rinse the shrimp under cold running water and pat dry.

2. In a large bowl, whisk the Basil Oil, ginger, Chili Oil, and scallions.

3. Add the shrimp to the bowl and let marinate 30 minutes at room temperature.

4. Heat a large sauté pan over medium heat. Add the shrimp and marinade and sauté 3 minutes.

5. Add the jalapeño peppers and sauté 1 minute.

6. Add the baby bok choy and cook 3 minutes.

7. Remove the baby bok choy and place on serving plates, slightly spreading (fanning) their leaves.

8. Spoon the shrimp over the baby bok choy.

9. Top with the sauce and serve.

Southwest Scented Tilapia

(Serves 4)

If you happen to be a seafood fan, you have probably seen a fish at your supermarket called tilapia. It is becoming quite popular and is rather inexpensive. It is rapidly becoming a favorite among chefs as it is a very versatile fish. So, logically, you may be wondering, "What is a tilapia?" Actually, it is a generic name for a species of cichlid fish and has been used for food since the days of the ancient Egyptians. Here in the great American Southwest, live tilapia are often used in waterways which are sources for drinking water as a way to keep the water pure from vegetation (algae) and parasites.

Tilapia fillets are about the same size as a catfish fillet, so you can count on one fillet per person when it comes to cooking and serving. As noted above, they are very versatile and can take any type of cooking from a simple and gentle sauté to a rough and rugged intense-heat grilling or broiling. In the case of Southwest Scented Tilapia, it is going to be pan fried (one of our favorite ways of preparing fish) and topped with a sauce laden with the flavors of the Southwest.

You will notice we serve fruit with this dish. Fruit with a main course is a very Southwest thing to do as we value our gardens and the robust harvest they give us. Here, we are going to use nectarines, but you can also use peaches as, botanically speaking, the only difference between the two fruits is their skin!

Ingredients
4 tilapia fillets
salt and pepper to taste
¼ cup Lemon Oil (page 32)
2 Tbs. butter
2 tsp. chili powder
2 tsp. cumin
2 scallions, minced
4 nectarines, peeled, pitted, and thinly sliced

Steps
1. Rinse the tilapia fillets under cold running water and pat dry.
2. Salt and pepper each tilapia fillet to taste.
3. In a large sauté pan, heat the Lemon Oil over medium heat.
4. Add the tilapia and sauté 5–7 minutes per side (depending on the thickness of the fillets).

5. Remove the tilapia to a platter and keep warm.
6. Into the sauté pan melt the butter over medium heat.
7. Stir in the chili powder, cumin, and scallions and cook 2 minutes.
8. Line the bottom of serving plates with the sliced nectarines.
9. Place the tilapia atop the nectarine.
10. Spoon the sauce over the tilapia and serve.

Stir Fry Mesa Shrimp

(Serves 4)

Even though the title of this dish has the words "stir fry" in it, it is not one of the many Southwest dishes which feature Asian undertones. The fact is, stir frying has been popular in the Southwest since before the states which make up this incredible part of America were even under United States control. Many Latin and South American countries stir fry because the term "stir fry" simply means to keep the food moving while it is being cooked.

Due to the fact that this dish does contain peppers and chili powder, it might be spicy hot to some tongues. There are two things you can do to take away some of the "heat." First, remove the seeds and white pithy membrane from the jalapeño peppers. Secondly, use a generic chili powder (there are various chili powders on the market with varying degrees of heat). You can also eliminate the chili powder altogether and simply use a sweet Hungarian paprika—you will keep the color of the dish, but the flavor will be greatly altered.

The best type of shrimp to be used for this dish are the medium-sized variety. They cook quickly, and their fresh flavor goes perfectly with the other ingredients. If you want to get a little more "snazzy," you can use the large variety (usually referred to as prawns). If you do use the large variety, change the amount in the recipe to two pounds instead of the one pound for medium shrimp.

Ingredients

1 pound shrimp, peeled
¼ cup Basil Oil (page 28)
4 cloves garlic, peeled and minced
4 jalapeño peppers, minced
1 tsp. chili powder
1 Tbs. lemon juice

Steps

1. Rinse the shrimp under cold running water and pat dry.
2. In a wok or large sauté pan, heat the Basil Oil over medium-high heat.
3. Add the shrimp and stir fry 5 minutes (time may vary, depending on their size).

4. Add the garlic, jalapeño peppers, and chili powder and stir fry 2 minutes.

5. Add the lemon juice and give a few tosses to incorporate before serving.

Baja BLT Salad

(Serves 4)

If you happen to be over the age of forty, you well remember one of the best sandwiches ever created and a favorite at every café and coffee shop (real ones, not the ones of today) called a BLT. The letters "BLT," for you kids, stand for Bacon, Lettuce, and Tomato. To this very day, whenever I have one of these sandwiches, I think back to my mother and noshing on one of these at the old counters at the Woolworth stores. Here in the Southwest, we often pay homage to food memories, and this is how the Baja BLT Salad originated.

Of course it won't surprise you to learn that the Baja BLT Salad is a little spicier than the BLT sandwich you might be used to. Here we will have a wonderful dressing featuring a Serrano Chili Mayonnaise (page 22), and we have a touch of chili powder and garlic powder. We also bring a little more pizzazz to the final outcome with some sweet red onion. Though this salad does make a nice side salad for any meal, I really prefer it as a dinner salad with a freshly made pitcher of Sangria (page 309–311).

There are two smoked types of bacon which will make this salad truly memorable. First, you can use an Applewood-smoked bacon which is readily available at all supermarkets. You can also use mesquite-smoked bacon, which you would have to search for or make yourself. If you want to add a little spice to the salad, peppered bacon would work well too.

Ingredients

1 pound smoked bacon, cooked
½ cup Serrano Chili Mayonnaise (page 22)
1 tsp. chili powder
½ tsp. garlic powder
1 head lettuce, any leafy variety
8 Roma tomatoes, sliced
2 small sweet red onions, peeled and thinly sliced

Steps

1. Cut each slice of cooked bacon into 4 pieces.
2. In a medium bowl, whisk the Serrano Chili Mayonnaise, chili powder, and garlic powder.
3. Line 4 serving plates with lettuce leaves, tomatoes, and onions.

4. Place the bacon atop the vegetables.
5. Spoon some dressing over the bacon and serve.

Cornbread Salad with Homemade Ranch Dressing

(Serves 4)

Between the delicious cornbread of the southern region of the United States and the outrageously scrumptious cornbread of the American Southwest, I think we can safely say that a good cornbread is one of the most important elements of a tasty kitchen. I think a good cornbread also shows the cook loves you because, let's face a simple fact, cornbread will bring a smile and warmth to every living soul. In the southern regions of the United States, when there is leftover cornbread, they have some fantastic dishes they make with it. Here in the Southwest, we make a salad, but as you will soon find out, this is not your usual salad!

First of all, we have the Homemade Ranch Dressing. This is nothing like that industrial gunk you buy at the market. This is a fresh-tasting, satiny smooth, creamed dressing which has a flair of the Southwest thanks to the use of Gringo Mayonnaise (page 20). You can make this dressing ahead of time and keep it chilled until you are ready to use it.

Then there's the actual Cornbread Salad. You can use any type of cornbread you want for this salad. Personally, I think our High Desert Cornbread (page 198) really makes this salad special as it will also bring out the natural flavors in the Homemade Ranch Dressing.

For Homemade Ranch Dressing

¾ cup Gringo Mayonnaise (page 20)
¼ cup buttermilk
½ cup minced celery
2 Tbs. minced parsley or cilantro
1 Tbs. minced white onion
1 clove garlic, peeled and minced
¼ tsp. dried thyme, crumbled
¼ tsp. celery seeds
¼ tsp. salt
¼ tsp. ground black pepper

For Cornbread Salad

4 cups crumbled leftover cornbread
2 Roma tomatoes, chopped
8 green onions, chopped
6 radishes, thinly sliced
1 sweet green bell pepper, seeded and chopped
2 ears sweet corn (white or yellow), kernels only
¼ tsp. salt
½ tsp. ground black pepper

Steps

1. Place all of the Homemade Ranch Dressing ingredients into a medium bowl and whisk until smooth and creamy.

2. Spoon the dressing into a jar with an airtight lid and chill until ready to use.

3. Into a large bowl, combine and gently toss all of the Cornbread Salad ingredients.

4. Arrange the Cornbread Salad on a serving platter.

5. Spoon some of the Homemade Ranch Dressing over the salad.

6. Put the remaining Homemade Ranch Dressing in a bowl and serve alongside the salad.

Mexican Sweet Corn Salad

(Serves 4)

One of the great flavors of Mother Nature is the natural sweetness of sweet corn. It doesn't matter whether it is the yellow or white variety, there is no fresher sweetness than that of sweet corn. There is a vibrant crunch to each kernel. There is a stunning sweetness to the freshly hulled corn, and there, within the newly harvested cobs, is one of the most pure nectars in nature: the subtly sweet corn milk. It isn't officially summer in the Southwest until the first forkful of sweet corn enters our mouths.

Salads, for the most part, are a means to refresh one's mouth. This is the natural phenomenon which happens when you put freshly harvested vegetables in your mouth and start to chomp. Salads are an important part of the Southwest diet and really should be for everyone. They are a wonderful way to get your recommended allowances of nutrients (both vitamins and minerals), and in many cases the ingredients of salads are known disease-fighters. When it comes to eating, salads are really a win-win situation.

This salad is a seasonal salad as you only want to make it with freshly husked corn kernels. The frozen variety just doesn't have the flavor, and the canned varieties really shouldn't be eaten at all. Once you have removed the kernels from the corn, don't forget to take the back of your knife and scrape the cobs. This is where the corn milk is. Add the corn milk to the kernels for the utmost in taste. This salad does call for raspberry vinegar, which is available in all supermarkets. If you prefer not to use raspberry vinegar, then apple cider vinegar will work fine—but nothing more acidic than that, or it will overpower the flavors of the salad.

Ingredients

4 ears sweet corn (white or yellow), husked
2 cups chopped tomatoes
1 tsp. salt
½ tsp. ground black pepper
¼ cup olive oil
2 Tbs. raspberry vinegar
2 shallots, peeled and minced
1 green onion, minced
2 cloves garlic, peeled and minced
¼ cup minced cilantro

Steps

1. Remove the kernels from the corn and scrape the cobs for the corn milk.
2. Into a large bowl, combine the corn kernels, tomatoes, salt, and pepper.
3. In a medium bowl, whisk the olive oil, raspberry vinegar, shallots, green onion, garlic, and cilantro.
4. Pour the dressing over the corn salad and toss.
5. Serve the Mexican Sweet Corn Salad at room temperature for the best in flavor.

Bacon Cheddar Salad

(Serves 4)

As you will find out, we Southwesterners don't think of salads as a bunch of green leaves tossed on a plate. We call that rabbit food. We also don't drench our salads in industrial-strength gunk called salad dressing. In the Southwest, a salad is something to be enjoyed and relished. In some instances, our salads are served warm, and in many instances, our salads can often be served as a main course (as we often do during the summer months).

Here in the great American Southwest, we love our cheeses, and we have many artisan cheesemakers. One of our favorites is cheddar cheese (even though it originated in England), and oftentimes you will find us using a white cheddar cheese, which is originally how it was made before dye was added to make it an orange color. Another of our favorite foods is smoked bacon, and if you were to venture into the backyards of many homes in the Southwest, you would see a smoker of one type or another sitting there. When you put these two staples of the Southwest kitchen together, you can come up with quite a delicious and interesting creation, just like this Bacon Cheddar Salad.

Any type of smoked bacon will work wonderfully for this dish. Here in the Southwest, we prefer Applewood- or mesquite-smoked bacon. Applewood-smoked bacon, you can find at most markets. Mesquite-smoked bacon, you usually have to smoke yourself (unfortunately). To get the full flavor of this salad, you do want to make it just before you serve it, as you want the heat from the bacon to slightly melt the cheese.

Ingredients

1 pound smoked bacon, chopped
½ pound cheddar cheese, grated
1 white onion, peeled and minced
2 Tbs. Red Chili Sauce (page 59)
1 head lettuce, the leafy variety

Steps

1. In a large sauté pan over medium heat, cook the bacon to your desired doneness.

2. In a large bowl, combine the cheddar cheese, onion, and Red Chili Sauce.

3. Remove the bacon from the pan with a slotted spoon and gently toss with the cheese mixture.

4. Spoon onto plates lined with lettuce leaves and serve immediately (the heat from the bacon will slightly melt the cheese).

Santa Fe Carrot Salad

(Serves 4)

The lowly carrot salad. The Rodney Dangerfield of salads. The salad everyone scoffed at during family gatherings or church socials. It was always pretty to look at. It was bright and enchanting, but it was . . . well, it was boring. Then the carrot salad came to the Southwest and received a makeover, and once you try Santa Fe Carrot Salad, you will truly understand the meaning of the term "naturally delicious!"

When it comes to carrot salad, should it be shredded or grated? This is really a matter of taste (and quite obviously texture). Personally, I prefer grated as I think the carrots are more flavorful this way, and in the case of Santa Fe Carrot Salad, I think it goes much better with the other ingredients. I also believe that the grated carrots blend much better with the dressing which accompanies this salad.

This dish does call for julienned dates (cut into long thin strips). The mere thought of cutting dried fruits and dates sends quivers up the spines of many people because all the damn things do is stick to the knife. There is a remedy for this. Dust the dates or dried fruit with some cornstarch or rice flour before you begin to chop them, and the fruit will not stick to the knife. There, problem solved!

Ingredients

1 pound carrots, peeled
1 pound cherries, pitted and halved
1 cup dates, pitted and julienned (cut into long thin strips)
½ cup pumpkin seeds
1 cup Gringo Mayonnaise (page 20)
¼ cup raw honey

Steps

1. Using either a box grater or the grating blade on your food processor, grate the carrots.
2. Place the grated carrots into a large bowl.
3. Stir in the cherries, dates, pumpkin seeds, Gringo Mayonnaise, and raw honey.
4. Let the Santa Fe Carrot Salad sit at room temperature for 30 minutes.
5. If not serving right away, chill until ready to serve.

Sautéed Prawn and Portobello Salad

(Serves 4)

As anyone who lives in an area where you have hot summers will attest to, there is no better meal on a sizzling summer evening than a salad. It is light, refreshing, and resupplies your body with the vitamins and minerals you've depleted during the day. Lounging out on the patio or deck with a delicious salad makes summers even more enjoyable.

Sautéed Prawns and Portobello Salad is a summer dinner salad to be cherished. You have lovely large prawns (big shrimp) and tender juicy portobello mushrooms. You also have some slight spiciness and a touch of sweet acidity with the raspberry vinegar. Enjoy this salad with a nice pitcher of sangria, and it will almost be as if every single worry in your life disappears with each forkful of this delicious delight.

Now you might be wondering, what is the difference between a prawn and a shrimp? To simplify that question, a prawn is a large shrimp. In many cases, this can be a freshwater shrimp, which can be quite large (and rather expensive). You can always substitute shrimp for prawns as they have just about the same cooking time, depending on size. You will want to use only large portobello mushrooms for this dish. The good news here is that you can either slice the portobello mushrooms yourself, or most markets will sell portobello mushrooms already sliced (which I actually do not recommend as they are often quite tough since they have been sliced days or weeks ago).

Ingredients

1 pound prawns or large shrimp

¼ cup butter

½ cup olive oil

4 large portobello mushrooms (or 8 medium), thickly sliced

1 white onion, peeled and thinly sliced

4 cloves garlic, peeled and thinly sliced

1 tsp. ground cumin

2 tsp. Chili Oil (page 29)

4 tomatoes, sliced

¼ cup raspberry vinegar

Steps

1. Rinse the prawns under cold running water and pat dry.
2. In a large sauté pan over medium heat, melt the butter into the olive oil.
3. Place the prawns into the sauté pan and sauté 3–5 minutes per side (depending on their size).
4. Remove the prawns from the pan and set aside.
5. Into the sauté pan, add the mushrooms and sauté 3 minutes per side.
6. Remove the mushrooms from the pan and set aside.
7. Into the sauté pan, combine the onion, garlic, cumin, and chili oil and cook 3 minutes.
8. Frame the serving plates with the sliced tomatoes.
9. Arrange the mushrooms on the serving plates.
10. Place the shrimp atop the mushrooms and drizzle the sauce from the pan.
11. Sprinkle the salads with the raspberry vinegar and serve.

Seared Steak Salad

(Serves 4)

Probably the most famous salad in the world featuring beef is the famed Black-and-Blue Salad, and I will share with you our Southwest version of this this salad on page 162. I think if more people visited the Southwest and tried our various salads featuring beef, this type of salad would be more popular. These salads make for a wonderful dinner, and they contain every nutritional element your body requires from a healthy dinner— and for the most part, they are low fat. It's a win-win situation.

Seared Steak Salad defines the word "scrumptious." It is also very simple to make, and you can do this either on your outdoor grill or inside with a grill pan. Can't get much more simple than that, now can it?

What you want here is very thinly sliced portions of beef. You do want to make sure the beef is "marbled," meaning there is fat running through it, for the very simple reason that fat means flavor. At Casa de Cuisine, we like to use thinly sliced tri-tip to make our Seared Steak Salad. You only want your beef on the heat for a very short period of time as thinly cut beef can become tough very fast.

When it comes to a salad such as this, lettuce is actually quite important. You want something rather dainty or leafy. Stay away from the iceberg types of lettuce as they are really good for nothing but a filling for tacos and the like. Bibb or butter lettuce is a little too fragile, and the texture will clash with the beef. The best lettuce would be a red leaf lettuce or romaine.

Ingredients

1 pound thinly sliced beef
salt and pepper to taste
2 tsp. Cumin Oil (page 31)
1 tsp. garlic powder
2 tsp. Worcestershire sauce
1 Tbs. Roasted Garlic Sauce (page 61)
2 tsp. steak sauce
1 head red leaf lettuce.
2 jalapeño peppers, minced
2 shallots, peeled and thinly sliced
2 tomatoes, chopped

Steps

1. Chop the beef and then season it with the salt and pepper.
2. In a large sauté pan, heat the Cumin Oil over medium heat.
3. Add the beef and cook 5 minutes (time may vary, depending on thinness).
4. Into the pan, add the garlic powder, Worcestershire sauce, Roasted Garlic Sauce, and steak sauce and cook 2 minutes.
5. Remove the pan from the heat.
6. Mound some lettuce leaves on each serving plate.
7. Mound the steak atop the lettuce. The heat from the steak will naturally wilt the lettuce a little.
8. Top the steak with some jalapeño peppers and shallots.
9. Frame the salad with some tomatoes and serve.

Southwest Black-and-Blue Salad

(Serves 4)

Salad aficionados know the Black-and-Blue Salad well. It is a classic and on the menu at some of the finest restaurants in the world. It is a wondrous blend of tastes and textures and one of those salads you wish will never end once you start eating it. Its name is derived from the fact that it contains Black Angus beef and bleu cheese. Pretty simple, when you think about it. Here in the great American Southwest, we have our own version of this salad, and as you might expect, it is different yet still pays a tasty homage to the original.

The main difference between the Southwest Black-and-Blue Salad and the original is that ours does not contain beef! The "black" in our version comes from black beans, a Southwest favorite. The "blue" in our version does come from bleu cheese, but this is where the comparisons end. What do we use for the meat instead of beef? We use a smoked bacon. If you can find a mesquite-smoked bacon, by all means, use that. If not, an applewood-smoked bacon will fit the bill perfectly.

Our dressing for this is not the usual industrial creamed gunk used on most salads of this ilk. We are going to use a Basil Oil with a raspberry vinegar. Very refreshing. You can make your own Basil Oil by using my recipe on page 28. If you are not a fan of cilantro (of which I cannot imagine), you can use a flat-leaf parsley instead; the overall Southwest flavor of the salad will indeed be diminished, but it will still be quite good.

Ingredients

1 15-ounce can black beans
2 Roma tomatoes, chopped
4 shallots, peeled and minced
¼ cup minced cilantro
½ cup Basil Oil (page 28)
¼ cup raspberry vinegar
¼ pound bacon, cooked and chopped
¼ cup bleu cheese, crumbled

Steps

1. Place the beans into a colander and rinse under cold, running water.

2. In a large bowl, combine the beans, tomatoes, shallots, and cilantro.

3. In a small bowl, whisk the Basil Oil and raspberry vinegar.
4. Pour the dressing over the bean mixture and toss to blend.
5. Let the bean mixture sit at room temperature 30 minutes.
6. Add the bacon and cheese and gently toss.
7. Serve over a bed of tender greens.

Sweet Potato Salad

(Serves 4)

Is there a more American salad than potato salad? Okay, maybe that is not really fair since potato salad came here from Germany, but I think you get my drift. Every time I chomp into a freshly made potato salad, I become immersed in memories. There was not a single summer in my young life when my mother did not have a potato salad in the refrigerator. Potato salad truly is one of the great comfort foods of all time, but like all good and great things, sometimes you need to change them to fit the times . . . thus enter Sweet Potato Salad.

Sweet potatoes are a very popular crop here in the Southwest, and many people have them sprouting up in their home gardens. They are indeed rather easy to grow, and of course, their health benefits are enormous. If you have never had a Sweet Potato Salad, I think you are in for a very happy experience. You'll still have that yummy, creamy goodness, but instead of sinking your teeth into a boring and blasé white potato, it will be sweet potatoes.

This Sweet Potato Salad is the epitome of a savory salad. Just one look at the ingredients will tell you this is truly something special. It, of course, has a slight sweetness to it with the sweet potatoes, raspberry vinegar, and the glazed pecans, but it also has the flavorful spices the Southwest is known for—and though you see a lot of different chili peppers associated with some of the ingredients, it is not really spicy hot.

Ingredients

4 sweet potatoes, peeled and cubed

4 jalapeño peppers, minced

4 green onions, chopped

½ cup Chipotle Mayonnaise (page 16)

½ cup Serrano Chili Mayonnaise (page 22)

2 Tbs. Basil Oil (page 28)

2 Tbs. Maple Dill Mustard (page 19)

2 Tbs. raspberry vinegar

2 cups chopped, glazed pecans or walnuts

Steps

1. Place the potatoes into a pot of boiling water and cook until fork tender.
2. Drain the potatoes and discard the cooking liquid.
3. Into a large bowl, combine the potatoes, jalapeño peppers, and green onions.
4. In a medium bowl, whisk the Chipotle Mayonnaise, Serrano Chili Mayonnaise, Basil Oil, Maple Dill Mustard, and raspberry vinegar until smooth.
5. Spoon the dressing over the sweet potatoes and gently toss.
6. Chill the Sweet Potato Salad until ready to serve.
7. Just before serving, top with the glazed pecans.

Whiskey Grilled Portobello Salad

(Serves 4)

There is fungus among us! Mushrooms are becoming quite popular these days and for very good reason. They are loaded with minerals and vitamins. They are rather inexpensive. They are a great alternative to meat. They are one of the most versatile food products on the entire planet. Oh yeah, they are also pretty damn delicious! This salad, featuring baby portobello mushrooms (and whiskey), I am sure will become a staple in your salad repertoire.

We have dealt with portobellos a lot in this book as they are one of the most popular mushrooms in Southwest cuisine. For this salad, we will be using baby portobello mushrooms. As you may have guessed, they are smaller than large portobello mushrooms. In many instances, smaller means more flavorful. This is not really the case with mushrooms. We use the smaller variety for this salad solely for the ease of eating the salad. Baby portobello mushrooms taste just like their larger counterpart.

What really sets this salad apart is that it is served over baby spinach leaves and beansprouts. This is simply a wonderful combination of both taste and texture and greatly enhances the flavor of the mushrooms. The one thing you want to always remember about beansprouts is they are very susceptible to bacteria. When buying them at the market, always check the expiration date. When you get them home, always rinse them under cold running water and keep what you don't use in a zip-lock bag. Do not use them past three days once you have opened their package.

Ingredients

1 pound baby portobello mushrooms, stems removed
2 tsp. garlic powder
2 tsp. garlic salt
1 tsp. ground black pepper
1 lime, juice only
¼ cup whiskey
3 Tbs. Worcestershire sauce
3 Tbs. steak sauce
vegetable oil
baby spinach leaves
beansprouts

Steps

1. Using a damp cloth, wipe off any excess dirt from the mushrooms.
2. In a large bowl, whisk the garlic powder, garlic salt, black pepper, lime juice, whiskey, Worcestershire sauce, and steak sauce.
3. Place the mushrooms into the marinade, toss to coat, and let marinate 30 minutes at room temperature.
4. Pre-heat your grill or a grill pan.
5. Once hot, brush the grill or grill pan with vegetable oil.
6. Place the mushrooms, cap-side-up, on the grill or grill pan and grill 3–5 minutes (depending on their size).
7. Turn the mushrooms over. Spoon some of the marinade into the crevices of the mushrooms and grill 3 minutes.
8. Mound some spinach leaves onto the serving plates.
9. Place some beansprouts atop the spinach leaves.
10. Place the mushrooms on top of the beansprouts and serve.

Whiskey Cherry Salad

(Serves 4)

Usually when you have a fruit salad, you get a plate with some pretty colored fruit on it and maybe, just maybe, a substance which seems to be creamy and is like a dressing. The fruit may taste good, but for the most part, the whole thing is really pretty boring. In the Southwest, we don't do boring. We abhor boring. Boring is not a word allowed in our kitchens. We do, however, do a fruit salad, and we call it Whiskey Cherry Salad.

For the best in taste and texture, this is a seasonal dish as it really comes alive when cherries are in season. If you do get a hankering for this salad during the winter months when cherries are hard to come by, you can use the organic cherries which come in cans and are usually called "sour" cherries (even though they are not really sour at all).

This recipe for Whiskey Cherry Salad is how I make it at Casa de Cuisine. You can, of course, use other fruits, but I think the ones we use not only show off the flavors of the Southwest (yes, we do grow bananas and mangoes here) but the colors also scream out Southwest. The whiskey used in this salad will not be diluted, so you will be getting the full amount of alcohol. With this noted, this should not be served to any family or friends with alcohol-related illnesses.

Ingredients

1 pound cherries, pitted and halved
⅓ cup whiskey
4 mangoes, peeled, pitted, and cubed
¼ tsp. ground nutmeg
4 bananas, peeled and quartered lengthwise
1 tsp. poppy seeds

Steps

1. Place the cherries into a large bowl and pour the whiskey over them.
2. Let the cherries macerate (soak) in the whiskey 30 minutes at room temperature.
3. Into the bowl, stir the mangoes and nutmeg.
4. Arrange the bananas on a serving platter.
5. Spoon the cherry mixture over the bananas.
6. Sprinkle the Whiskey Cherry Salad with poppy seeds and serve.

Chilled Cherry Soup

(Serves 4)

First of all, this is a seasonal soup. You only want to make this soup when cherries are in season, but the good news here is, cherries are now in season almost nine months during the course of the year thanks to the growing season in South and Central America. The reason you do not want to use the organic canned variety of cherries for this soup is their texture. They just do not have the "bite" to make this soup as special as it is.

In most cases when you have a dish served cold featuring fruit, you do not want to chill the fruit because it will dull the natural flavors of the fruit. This is not the case with this soup since we will be cooking the cherries (they won't be raw). Cooking the cherries will make somewhat of a natural syrup, which will be the base of the soup, and it will also bring out the stunning color of the soup, which, surprise, will be a dark cherry red.

This soup does contain wine. You will want to use a dry red wine for the simple reason that you do not want that much floral or fruity flavor to the wine, or it will take away from the flavor of the cherries. This is a wonderful soup for the summer months, and I will usually prepare it and have it on the table whenever I am grilling or barbecuing out on the patio.

Ingredients

1 pound cherries, pitted and halved
3½ cups water
½ cup sugar
2 Tbs. arrowroot
1 cup dry red wine

Steps

1. In a medium, non-aluminum saucepan, combine the cherries, water, and sugar over medium heat and bring to a boil.

2. Reduce the heat to a simmer and cook 10 minutes.

3. In a small bowl, whisk the arrowroot and ¼ cup of the cherry cooking liquid.

4. Whisk the arrowroot mixture back into the cherries and cook 3 minutes (it will thicken).

5. Into the soup, stir the wine and cook 2 minutes.

6. Remove the pan from the heat and let cool to room temperature.

7. Chill the soup at least 2 hours before serving.

Chilled Sherry and Avocado Soup

(Serves 4)

Chilled soups are a wonderful way to build your repertoire of soup recipes, and they are simply a godsend on those hot and sometimes humid summer days here in the Southwest. There is nothing quite like relaxing out on the deck or patio with a loaf of artisan bread, a pitcher of sangria, and a bowl of a delicious chilled soup. If you are going to make that soup your dinner, it is rather important to have some "fat" in the soup because, whether you want to admit it or not, we do need fat in our diet because without it . . . we die!

Chilled Sherry and Avocado Soup is quite a rich soup as you might be able to tell from the ingredients, and for this reason, you do want the portions to be smaller than usual. When it comes to picking out the avocados for this soup, you do want them to be ripe because you want to mash them with a fork and not puree them in a food processor. The mashing with a fork is important for the texture of the soup.

Regarding the "fat" in this soup. It basically comes from the heavy cream, which will give the soup its richness and silky texture. You can use half-and-half if you must cut down on fat, but it will take away from the richness and texture. What you do not want to use, however, is milk. Using milk will make the soup too thin (runny) and basically ruin it.

Ingredients

2 large avocados, peeled and pitted
1 cup heavy cream
3 cups chicken stock
¼ cup sherry
1 tsp. salt
1 jalapeño pepper, minced

Steps

1. Place the avocados into a large bowl and mash them with the tines of a fork.
2. Into the avocados, stir in the cream until well blended.
3. In a medium saucepan over medium heat, bring the chicken stock to a simmer.
4. Into the chicken stock, whisk in the avocado mixture, sherry, and salt and cook 5 minutes. Do not let it come to a boil, or the cream may separate.

5. Remove the pan from the heat and let cool to room temperature.
6. Place the soup in the refrigerator and chill until ready to serve.
7. Ladle into bowl, top with some jalapeño pepper, and serve.

Casa Chili Soup

(Serves 4)

I often get asked, what is the difference between a chili and a soup? It is a good question and one without a feasible answer, yet I suppose the most logical answer would be: a chili will have chili peppers in it whereas a soup might not. Perhaps it might also have to do with the thickness. Most chilis can almost be eaten with a fork whereas soups need a spoon. Or maybe we all just overthink things too damn much and should just enjoy the bowl of chili or soup which is in front of us and quit asking questions!

Casa Chili Soup is, without a doubt, one of my favorite soups no matter what time of year. It is the perfect fusion of a chili and a soup. It is loaded with nutritional goodness, and if you serve it with some freshly made flour tortillas, it is a complete meal. This version of Casa Chili Soup does contain beans. If you are not a fan of beans, just don't put them in, but remember, beans are one of the best foods you can put into your body. I like to use pinto beans, but you can actually use any type of bean. If you are using a canned bean, remember to rinse them before using them.

The vegetables I use in this recipe are all native to the great American Southwest. You can use whatever your favorite vegetables are, and when it comes to the meat, you can use either pork or beef. I think beef gives the soup a better flavor. If you do use pork, remember to trim off any excess fat, and to add some extra flavor, you can toss in a few slices of smoked bacon (chopped up).

Ingredients

3 Tbs. Chili Oil (page 29), divided
2 pounds lean beef, cubed
1 white onion, peeled and chopped
2 carrots, peeled and chopped
2 stalks celery, chopped
4 cloves garlic, peeled and minced
1 Tbs. chili powder
1 Tbs. dried oregano, crumbled
7 cups beef stock
4 Roma tomatoes, chopped
¼ cup chopped flat-leaf parsley
1 16-ounce can pinto beans, drained and rinsed (optional)

Steps

1. In a large sauté pan, heat 2 Tbs. of the Chili Oil over medium heat.
2. Add the beef and brown on all sides.
3. Remove the beef and set aside.
4. In the sauté pan, heat the remaining Chili Oil over medium heat.
5. Add the onion, carrots, celery, and garlic and sauté 5 minutes.
6. Stir in the chili powder and oregano and cook 2 minutes.
7. Add the beef, beef stock, tomatoes, and parsley and bring to a boil.
8. Reduce the heat to a simmer and cook 1 hour.
9. Add the beans and cook 10 minutes.
10. Ladle into bowls and serve.

··· Note ···

If you prefer a slightly thicker soup, just stir in a tablespoon or two of yellow cornmeal about ten minutes before the soup is done.

Sherry Sprouts

(Serves 4)

Look, a dish featuring Brussels sprouts! Don't you dare turn the page. Brussels sprouts are a great vegetable and not just because they are so nutritional and loaded with vitamins and minerals but because they taste good . . . when properly prepared. The reason why most people do not like Brussels sprouts is because they grew up with them being overcooked. I know, because I am one of these people. I hated these embryonic cabbages. Then I learned how to cook them. Now I love them. What is the secret to cooking Brussels sprouts? Two secrets: first, remove the core; second, barely cook them.

When Brussels sprouts are overcooked, they release a sulfuric chemical compound with makes them stink and gives them a terrible flavor. Many types of cabbage do the same thing. Brussels sprouts should never be boiled. Matter of fact, I would go far as to say they should not ever be steamed. There are only two ways Brussels sprouts should ever be cooked: either sautéed or grilled. If sautéed, then only for a few minutes. If grilled, brushed with a seasoned oil and grilled for a very short time. I have turned many Brussels sprouts haters into lovers with Sherry Sprouts.

We are going to use a sherry for this dish, but if you're not a fan of sherry or find it too expensive, you can use a sweet port wine. We are going to finish this incredible side dish with some Asiago cheese, which will give the final product a nice little "nutty" flavor. Even though this dish does have cheese which will be melted, it is not considered an "au gratin" dish.

Ingredients
1 pound Brussels sprouts
2 Tbs. rendered bacon fat (fat from cooked bacon)
4 cloves garlic, peeled and minced
½ cup chopped cooked bacon
1 tsp. Chili Oil (page 29)
½ cup sherry
1 cup finely grated Asiago cheese

Steps
1. Remove the tough outer leaves of the Brussels sprouts and then remove the core.
2. Using a sharp knife, shred the Brussels sprouts.

3. In a medium sauté pan, heat the bacon fat over medium heat. Add the Brussels sprouts and sauté 5 minutes.

4. Add the garlic, bacon, Chili Oil, and sherry and sauté 2 minutes.

5. Place the Sherry Sprouts onto a serving dish, top with the cheese, and serve.

Spiced Latin Hushpuppies

(Makes about 14, depending on size)

Hushpuppies! If you're not from the South, you might only think hushpuppies are a brand name of a shoe from days gone by. In fact, hushpuppies are an incredible fried bread, usually on the savory side, and once you start eating them, it is very difficult to stop. By the way, I have no idea why they are called hushpuppies. Here in the Southwest, we have our own version of hushpuppies, and we serve them with a variety of sauces as a side dish during our summer grilling and barbecue parties.

To perfectly cook (fry) hushpuppies, you must pay attention to the oil. It is very important if you don't want to end up serving globs of coagulated grease. You will need a deep-fry thermometer. They are very inexpensive and a must-have. You want to place your hushpuppies into the oil when it reaches 350°F. What will happen is, as soon as the hushpuppies hit the hot oil, they will crust over. This means the oil will not get into the batter, and due to the crusting, the inside of the hushpuppies will cook by steam. Basic Food Science 101.

These are savory hushpuppies and not spicy hot ones. If you want to make them spicy hot, use a different pepper. If you are a fan of hushpuppies, you might notice we don't use the usual onions here. The reason is simple. Onions contain too much liquid, and I find the hushpuppies become too dense. You will find these hushpuppies are lighter than usual. Only fry your hushpuppies in either corn oil or peanut oil. Do not use an olive oil, or you might cause a fire (olive oil will breakdown with a very high heat).

Ingredients

1 cup yellow cornmeal
1½ cups flour
1 tsp. baking powder
1 tsp. salt
1 Tbs. sugar
1 egg
1 cup milk
1 jalapeño pepper, minced
2 cloves garlic, peeled and minced
1 Tbs. Red Chili Sauce (page 59)
corn oil, for frying

Steps

1. In a large bowl, whisk the cornmeal, flour, baking powder, salt, and sugar.

2. In a medium bowl, whisk the egg, milk, jalapeño pepper, garlic, and Red Chili Sauce.

3. Stir the egg mixture into the flour to make a batter.

4. Let the batter rest 10 minutes.

5. In a large sauté pan or deep skillet, heat enough oil to deep-fry and bring to 350°F on a deep-fry thermometer.

6. Carefully add the batter by the tablespoon into the hot oil and fry until golden.

7. With a slotted spoon, remove the hushpuppies to a paper towel–lined plate to drain off excess oil.

8. Let cool before serving.

··· Note ···

If you make your hushpuppies too thick, they will not cook internally and you will bite into gunk. Not good! Use two tablespoons to plop them into the oil. One tablespoon with the batter and the other to push it off the spoon and into the oil.

Kahlúa Creamed Corn

(Serves 4)

Due to the climate and soil structure, some of the best sweet corn in the world is grown in the great American Southwest. This should really not surprise anyone when you consider this part of America is known for their corn dishes and the cuisines which have inspired the food of the Southwest are known for their culinary creations featuring maize (corn). If you ever get the chance to pull an ear of corn off a stalk, pull back the husk, and take a big juicy bite, by all means, do, and taste the naturally sweet side of Mother Nature.

To make Kahlúa Creamed Corn, you want to use only freshly shucked corn. To shuck corn is very simple. Take the ear of corn and pull back and remove the husk. Then take the corn silk (strands) and pull them off. Take a sharp knife and run it down the corn to remove the kernels. Then take the back of the knife (non-sharp part of the blade) and scrape the corn cob to remove the sweet corn milk. It is that easy.

This is a naturally creamed corn. It will not have the same consistency as that gunk you buy in cans, which has multiple thickeners in it. What you will be tasting here is pure and natural, and as a taste bonus, you'll get some Kahlúa!

Ingredients

4 ears of corn, shucked (see note above)
2 Tbs. heavy cream
2 jalapeño peppers, minced
½ sweet red bell pepper, seeded and minced
4 shallots, peeled and minced
1 tsp. salt
½ cup Kahlúa
2 Tbs. minced cilantro

Steps

1. In a medium sauté pan over medium heat, combine the corn (and corn milk) and cream and bring just to a simmer.

2. Stir in the jalapeño peppers, bell pepper, shallots, and salt and cook 4 minutes.

3. Remove the pan from the heat and stir in the Kahlúa.

4. Place the pan back on the heat and cook 1 minute.

5. Spoon the Kahlúa Creamed Corn into a serving bowl, top with the cilantro, and serve.

Mexican Medallions of Corn

(Serves 4)

More than a few years back, I was asked to come up with a dish featuring corn on the cob which could be enjoyed by people who wear dentures. No, I am serious. My first thought was, "huh?" Then I began to think about it and realized there was a way for people with dentures (or bad teeth) to eat corn on the cob . . . if I could somehow shorten the cob. I did. The dish was a hit, even with people who could eat corn on the cob. That dish was Mexican Medallions of Corn.

To prepare the corn for this dish is quite simple. All you need is a sharp, heavy knife. After you shuck the corn (remove the husk and corn silk), you simply cut it into 1-inch portions (medallions). This way, it takes very little pressure for the mouth to remove the kernels from the cob, and you get the full flavor of the cob itself. Of course, the way it is cooked also gives the corn a lot of flavor.

The cooking process here is rather elementary. Since corn is fresher-tasting when it is barely cooked, we are only going to essentially heat the corn to the point where the other flavors will meld with it, and the other flavors are simply two Southwest favorites: jalapeño pepper and green onion. What will bind these flavors is butter. As the adage goes: "Easy peasy!"

Ingredients
4 ears sweet corn, yellow or white
½ cup butter
2 jalapeño peppers, minced
1 green onion, minced

Steps
1. Cut the cobs of corn into medallions (see note above).
2. In a large sauté pan, melt the butter over medium heat.
3. Add the jalapeño peppers and green onion and sauté 2 minutes.
4. Add the corn and sauté 4 minutes per side.
5. Remove the medallions of corn and place on a serving platter.
6. Spoon the butter sauce over the corn and serve.

Picante Potatoes

(Serves 4)

The history of the potato is a wonderful history. It is a food which has kept people alive through very bad times. It is the fourth largest food crop in the world. It has withstood droughts and all the calamities Mother Nature could throw at it. Yes, that basic brown globular thing in your kitchen truly is a wonder. There are many different varieties of potatoes on the market today, and more are being developed via science. In the case of this dish, Picante Potatoes, we will be using the lovely Yukon Gold potatoes, and you can find them in all supermarkets.

In the world of food, Yukon Gold potatoes are a mere baby. They were not brought onto the market until 1980. If you have never had a Yukon Gold potato, you might be interested in the fact that they have a slight sweetness to them and are moister when raw than a usual potato. They are also a rather versatile potato which can take roasting, frying, and grilling. For this dish, they are going to be roasted, and due to their texture, they will take in all the flavors of the herbs and spices they will be roasted with.

In this dish, we are going to be using a rather famous vegetable here in the Southwest: a leek. Many people are turned off by leeks because they claim their texture is too tough. This is not the case when they are properly prepared. To use a leek, you want to remove the tough dark green top of the stalk. The only part of a leek you want to use (other than for a stock) is the tender white bottoms on up to the light green parts. You will find that, when cooked, these are very tender. By the way, you can grow leeks in your garden in most parts of the United States, and they are a wonderful winter crop.

Ingredients

1 pound Yukon Gold potatoes, unpeeled and cubed

¼ pound bacon, chopped

1 leek, chopped

4 cloves garlic, peeled and minced

½ cup Basil Oil (page 28)

6 basil leaves, chopped

1 tsp. celery seeds

1 Tbs. chili powder

½ tsp. salt

¼ tsp. ground black pepper

½ cup grated Asiago cheese

Steps

1. Into a large bowl, combine the potatoes, bacon, leek, garlic, Basil Oil, basil leaves, celery seeds, chili powder, salt, and pepper. Stir until blended.

2. Let the potato mixture sit for 30 minutes at room temperature.

3. Pre-heat your oven to 375°F.

4. Place the potato mixture into a roasting pan.

5. Place into the oven and roast 60 minutes (or until the potatoes are fork-tender). Stir the potatoes a few times during the cooking process.

6. Sprinkle the potatoes with the Asiago cheese and roast 10 additional minutes.

7. Remove from the oven and let cool slightly before serving.

··· Note ···

You can use Russet potatoes for this dish. You will just have to adapt the time. As long as they are fork-tender, it will be fine.

San Antonio Sautéed Mushrooms

(Serves 4)

Some dishes are just meant to accompany other dishes. It's like peaches and cream or oil and vinegar. When it comes to San Antonio Sautéed Mushrooms, they are the perfect side dish for any grilled or barbecued entrée, and if I was to be totally honest, I would admit that I have even eaten this luscious sherry-enriched fungi as an entrée themselves (but that would make me look gluttonous, and I refuse to do that).

Whereas we use mostly portobello mushrooms here in the Southwest, this dish actually tastes better if you use the simple "button" type of mushroom. What is a button mushroom? It is the little mushroom you see most often at the supermarket. When it comes to buying mushrooms of any type, you never want to buy them packaged—only loose—and there is a very good and scientific reason for this. Mushrooms are a living fungus, and they must be allowed to breathe to keep their maximum flavor. If they are in a package and covered with plastic, not only are they dying, they are very susceptible to bacteria.

This is a very simple side dish to prepare at home, and it is also very quick. You don't want to cook mushrooms for too long as they can get rubbery. Since any type of grilled or barbecued meat should be allowed to rest about 10 minutes after it has been cooked to retain its juices, once the meat is done, make your San Antonio Sautéed Mushrooms.

Ingredients

1 pound mushrooms, stem ends removed and sliced
¼ cup Cumin Oil (page 31)
2 Tbs. butter
2 shallots, peeled and minced
½ tsp. chili powder
½ cup sherry
½ tsp. salt
¼ tsp. ground black pepper

Steps

1. Using a damp cloth, wipe the mushrooms of any excess dirt.
2. In a large sauté pan, heat the Cumin Oil and butter over medium heat.

3. Add the shallots and sauté 3 minutes.
4. Stir in the chili powder and mushrooms and sauté 5 minutes.
5. Stir in the sherry, salt, and pepper. Lower the heat and cook 5 minutes.
6. Using a slotted spoon, place the mushrooms into a serving bowl.
7. Drizzle the mushrooms with the sauce and serve.

Yellow Split Pea Soup

(Serves 4)

Have you ever witnessed the beauty of a Southwest sunset? If not, you are missing out on one of the most incredible views that Mother Nature has to offer. The various shades of yellow, orange, and red are breathtaking. Whenever I make this classic Southwest version of split pea soup, I think about our sunsets because the colors of this soup are the colors of our sky.

What are split peas? They're peas that have had their skins removed, split in half, and dried. You might be wondering why some are green and some are yellow. They simply come from different species of the same family of plants. By the way, split peas and dhal come from two different legume species.

Anytime you are cooking with dried legumes (beans, split peas, etc.), it is going to take some time. It is time well worth spending as you can make a whole batch of this type of soup and then freeze what you don't use. This is a Southwest version of split pea soup, and here in the Southwest, we do like to use sausage in soups of this ilk. You can use any type of sausage you prefer, but the rule of thumb here is: the spicier the better. Since this is a creamed variety of soup, you can use either a food processor or blender to puree the soup, but be careful. Don't fill the machine with too much soup as the heat from the soup will create steam in the machine, and you can have a little explosion when you remove the top. Puree it in small batches.

Ingredients

1 16-ounce package of dried yellow split peas

7 cups chicken stock

8 ounces smoked sausage, casing removed and chopped

2 carrots, peeled and diced

4 shallots, peeled and minced

2 jalapeño peppers, diced

1 cup heavy cream

1 tsp. salt

½ tsp. ground black pepper

Steps

1. Pick over the split peas to remove any stones (there are often little stones or pebbles in the bag).

2. In a medium soup pot, bring the chicken stock to a boil over high heat. Add the split peas, lower the heat to a simmer, and cook 1 hour.

3. In a medium sauté pan over medium heat, brown the sausage.

4. Remove the sausage and set it aside (no need to drain on paper towels). Do not discard grease from the pan.

5. Into the sauté pan, add the carrots, shallots, and jalapeño peppers and sauté 5 minutes. If the sausage didn't render enough fat, add some olive oil.

6. Spoon the sautéed vegetables into the soup and cook 10 minutes.

7. Pour the soup, in batches, into a food processor or blender and puree. (Alternatively, you can use an immersion blender for this step, though it will take more time to puree everything.)

8. Pour the soup back into the pot and place over medium heat.

9. Stir in the sausage, cream, salt, and pepper and cook 5 minutes.

10. Ladle the soup into bowls and serve.

The Southwest Oven

Breads

Desserts

Bacon and Sweet Onion Bread

(Makes 2 loaves)

Smoked bacon and sweet onions, when paired together, are of one the great taste treats of all time. When you take these two flavors and combine them into a freshly baked artisan bread, you not only get one of the greatest breads to make a sandwich, but a bread you simply want to munch on.

This is a yeast-risen dough, so it will take some time from start to finish. One of the great things about Bacon and Sweet Onion Bread is that it resembles in texture some of the classic Italian breads. It has a soft crumb (dough) and the crust is solid enough to give you a nice delicate crunch when you bite into it. It is also a bread that is strong enough to handle saucy types of meat without falling apart—which makes it great for a hot sandwich.

The most time-consuming thing when making a yeast bread is the rising of the dough. Here is a little secret many breadmakers know: take an electric heating pad on the low setting and place the bowl of dough on the heating pad (make sure the bowl is tightly covered with plastic wrap, so the heat stays in the bowl). You can usually cut your rising time to about half (depending on the type of dough).

Ingredients
2½ tsp. yeast
¼ cup warm water
2 Tbs. sugar
1 cup warm milk
4½ cups flour, divided
½ cup chopped bacon
½ white onion, peeled and minced
1 tsp. salt

Steps
1. In a small bowl, whisk the yeast, water, and sugar. Set the bowl aside for the yeast to proof (foam).
2. In a large bowl, stir the milk and 2 cups of flour. (This is the dough.)
3. Into the dough, stir in the proofed yeast and set the bowl aside.

4. In a medium skillet over medium heat, cook the bacon, onion, and salt for 5 minutes.
5. Into the dough, stir the remaining flour and bacon mixture.
6. Place the dough on a floured surface and knead 10 minutes.
7. Place the dough into a bowl, cover, and let rise 2 hours.
8. Line the bottom of two 9x5-inch loaf pans with parchment paper.
9. Divide the dough into two portions and place into the prepared pans.
10. Let the dough rise in the pans 1 hour.
11. Pre-heat your oven to 400°F.
12. Place pans into the oven and bake 15 minutes.
13. Reduce the heat to 350°F and bake 35 minutes.
14. Remove the breads from the oven and let cool in the pan 10 minutes.
15. Remove the breads from the pans and let cool on a wire rack.

Buttermilk Biscuits

(Makes varying amounts, depending on biscuit size)

Oh come on, if you have never had homemade Buttermilk Biscuits, you cannot claim to be a true American. Buttermilk Biscuits are the quintessential American biscuit. They are delicious no matter how they are served, but for an absolute treat, at least a few of them must be slathered with fresh creamery butter and then drizzled with raw honey. Oh my lord, this is food bliss!

Here in the Southwest, we received our love of Buttermilk Biscuits from the delicious southern regions of the United States. As the great migration to the West was going on during the Dust Bowl and the Great Depression, many people from the southern states headed out this way to find a new life, and with them, they brought their family recipes and favorite dishes. This is actually how most regional cuisines come about—from local migration.

It should be pointed out that Buttermilk Biscuits do not freeze well once they have been baked (if there are any left over to freeze). Have no fear as you can freeze the prepared dough. Just shape the dough into biscuits and place them on a baking sheet. Put the baking sheet into the freezer and, once they are frozen, individually wrap them in plastic and place them into a zip-lock bag. Now you can have homemade Buttermilk Biscuits whenever your craving hits.

Ingredients

6 Tbs. butter, chilled
¼ cup lard
4 cups flour
¼ cup sugar
2 Tbs. baking powder
2 tsp. baking soda
2 tsp. salt
1¾ cups buttermilk

Steps

1. Pre-heat your oven to 400°F and line a baking sheet with parchment paper or a silicone baking sheet.
2. In a large bowl, combine the butter, lard, flour, sugar, baking powder, baking soda, and salt with a pastry blender (or pastry fork) until it is crumbly.
3. Stir in the buttermilk to make a dough.

4. Place the dough onto a floured surface and knead just until it comes together.

5. Re-flour the surface, roll out the dough to about 1½–2-inches thick, and with a round cookie cutter or biscuit cutter, cut out the biscuits.

6. Place the biscuits onto the prepared baking sheet.

7. Place into the oven and bake 15 minutes or until golden.

8. Remove from the oven and let cool on a wire rack.

Casa Vegan Cornbread

(Makes one 8-inch round cornbread)

When it comes to the world of cornbread, the varieties are limitless, and this is one of the great things about cornbread. I had never thought about cornbread being non-vegetarian until a friend of mine, who is vegan, mentioned he missed eating cornbread. Then I realized, traditional cornbread does contain quite a bit of dairy and, in some recipes, animal fat (bacon grease being one). Being the nice guy I am, I created this vegan style cornbread at Casa de Cuisine, so now everyone can enjoy the flavors of this American classic.

To truly understand baking, you must also have some knowledge of chemistry because, in reality, that is what baking is all about. It took me a while to conjure up this recipe because I had to replace fats (dairy) with non-fats and still have a cornbread which is flavorful and keeps its shape. Instead of milk or cream or buttermilk for this cornbread, we are going to use almond milk. Almonds contain enough fat and protein so that the almond milk will work. I wouldn't use soy or hemp milk for this dish, but you can use cashew milk (albeit this is a little more expensive). Make sure the almond milk you buy is organic and not flavored.

There is no need to do anything fancy when it comes to cornbread. Use the typical stone-ground yellow cornmeal and none of the chic cornmeal on the market. You'll just be wasting your money. If you are so inclined, you can use white cornmeal, but it just doesn't look as rich.

Ingredients

1 cup yellow cornmeal

1¼ cups flour

¼ cup brown sugar

1 Tbs. baking powder

½ tsp. baking soda

½ tsp. salt

1¼ cups almond milk

½ cup Cinnamon Oil (page 30)

2 Tbs. balsamic vinegar

Steps

1. Pre-heat your oven to 375°F. Line the bottom of an 8-inch round cake pan with parchment paper.

2. In a medium bowl, whisk the cornmeal, flour, brown sugar, baking powder, baking soda, and salt.

3. In a large bowl, whisk the almond milk, Cinnamon Oil, and balsamic vinegar.

4. Stir the cornmeal mixture into the almond milk mixture just until combined.

5. Let the batter rest 5 minutes.

6. Spoon the batter into the prepared cake pan.

7. Place into the oven and bake 20 minutes.

8. Remove the cornbread from the oven and let cool in the pan 10 minutes.

9. Remove the cornbread from the pan and let cool on a wire rack.

Cowboy Sweet Bread

(Makes 12 small breads)

Cowboy cooking is nothing new in the great American Southwest. Matter of fact, in many areas of the Southwest, cowboy cooking is a normal thing. If you were to do some research on cowboy cooking, you would be surprised to find that the origins of many of your favorite dishes are from these trailblazing men and women ("cowboy" was actually used as a generic word). What you don't hear about is the baking which was done on the trails. Yes, you can bake over an open fire. This Cowboy Sweet Bread is a little bit of tasty history, and we have adapted it so that you can make it at home without a campfire.

This is a yeast bread, so there will be a rising period. You might have noticed in cookbooks, when dealing with yeast, you are instructed to "proof the yeast." What this means is rather simple. You are proving the yeast is alive. Remember, yeast is an active culture (it lives). If the yeast is dead, your dough will not rise, and your bread will be ruined. When you proof yeast, it is always good to add some sugar or honey. The yeast will "eat" this, and you will get more foam.

This is called a "sweet" bread, but it is not overtly sweet like some breakfast breads called "sweet breads." The sweetness is slight and just plays with your tongue. This is one of the better breads to serve with anything featuring a barbecue sauce as the flavors will meld perfectly. You will be forming the dough into bun-shaped loaves.

Ingredients

1 cup warm milk
2¼ tsp. yeast
1 Tbs. honey
6 Tbs. melted butter
⅓ cup sugar
1 tsp. salt
2 eggs, beaten
4 cups flour

Steps

1. In a large bowl, whisk the warm milk, yeast, and honey. Set the bowl aside 10 minutes for the yeast to proof (foam).
2. Into the proofed yeast, whisk the butter, sugar, salt, and eggs.
3. Stir in the flour to form a dough.

4. Place the dough onto a floured surface and knead 5 minutes (this is a sticky dough so have some extra flour to coat your hands).

5. Place the dough back into the bowl and let it rise 90 minutes.

6. Remove the dough to a floured surface and divide into 12 pieces.

7. Roll each piece of dough into a ball.

8. Flatten each ball of dough, with your hands, to about ½-inch thickness.

9. Line two baking pans with parchment paper. Place the pieces of dough on the pans and let rise 30 minutes.

10. Pre-heat your oven to 350°F.

11. Place into the oven and bake 20 minutes.

12. Remove from the oven and let the Cowboy Sweet Bread cool on a wire rack.

Garlic and Smoked Gouda Bread

(Makes 2 loaves)

Whoever was the first person to think of smoking cheese deserves the Nobel Peace Prize for luxury eating. If you are a fan of cheese and you have never had the pleasure of munching on any smoked cheese, do yourself a favor right now. Put this book down and head to your market (if they have a good cheese section) and buy a few varieties of smoked cheese. They will become your heroin. Make sure one of them is a smoked Gouda so you can make this bread.

Breads laced with cheese are quite popular in the Southwest for the simple reason that cheese is quite popular and we look for all kinds of ways to include it in our diets. When you are using cheese in a bread, it is usually kneaded into the bread. This does cause a little bit more moisture in the dough, and the result is your crumb (dough) will be slightly more palatable. Of course, there is also the flavor factor, but the taste of the cheese will not overpower the bread itself. Then there is the garlic. Fear not, when garlic is baked into a product like bread, it is not strong in flavor as it loses quite a bit of its pungency. This is a good thing.

It is my opinion that, when you do add cheese to a bread, it should always be finely grated. Anything larger than a fine grade will clump in the dough. Once you have grated the cheese, toss it in a little flour or cornstarch. This will keep the cheese from sticking to itself and give you even distribution in the dough.

Ingredients

4½ cups flour

¼ cup sugar

2 tsp. yeast

1¾ cups warm water

1 Tbs. olive oil

5 cloves garlic, minced

1 cup finely grated smoked Gouda cheese

Steps

1. In a large bowl, stir the flour, sugar, yeast, water, and olive oil to form a dough.

2. Place the dough onto a floured surface and knead 5 minutes. The dough will be rather stiff.

3. Place the dough back into the bowl, cover, and let rise 1 hour.

4. Place the dough onto a floured surface and knead 5 minutes. Place back into the bowl and let rise 1 hour.

5. Place the dough onto a floured surface and flatten it out with your hands. Place the garlic and cheese on the dough and then fold the dough over upon itself. Knead the dough 5 minutes.

6. Line a baking sheet with parchment paper or a silicone baking sheet.

7. Divide the dough in half and with your hands, form each half into a long loaf.

8. Place the loaves on the prepared baking sheet and let rise 30 minutes.

9. Pre-heat your oven to 400°F.

10. Place the loaves into the oven and bake 25–30 minutes.

11. Remove the bread from the oven and let cool on a wire rack.

High Desert Cornbread

(Makes one 8-inch round cornbread)

The high desert regions of the American Southwest are some of the most beautiful places on earth. From the never-ending sky to the rolling dunes, your panoramic vision will take in all the beauty Mother Nature has bestowed upon us. From the sunrise of a new morning to the pastel sunset putting the high desert to sleep, each day is a new experience. And then there is the vibrant night sky, pitch black with the glistening of stars which seem so close you feel you can grab one. Ruggedly enchanting, the high desert of the great American Southwest is one of Earth's shining jewels, just as this High Desert Cornbread is one of the most savory cornbreads you will ever encounter.

Whereas many a cornbread is meant to be served with dishes featuring a sauce or gravy (the cornbread being a receptacle for these sauces and gravies), High Desert Cornbread is actually meant to be served next to the dish. Here we have a moist cornbread, as opposed to the usual cornbread texture of slight grittiness. Here we have a cornbread laden with the flavors of the Southwest, with each bite bringing a surprise to your mouth. In all actuality, High Desert Cornbread is really a nirvana for cornbread lovers from all walks of life.

This is our favorite cornbread at Casa de Cuisine and on the off-chance we have some left over, we also make a wonderful and simple appetizer with it. Simply take the cornbread and slice it in half. Spread each half with a little Chipotle Mayonnaise (page 16) and then layer some grated cheddar cheese on it. Place it into the oven until the cheese melts and enjoy! This would also be the perfect cornbread to make the Cornbread Salad (page 152).

Ingredients

¾ cup yellow cornmeal

¾ cup flour

¼ cup sugar

1½ tsp. baking powder

¾ tsp. baking soda

½ tsp. salt

1 cup sour cream

¼ cup minced green onions

2 jalapeño peppers, minced

2 Tbs. Cumin Oil (page 31)

2 Tbs. heavy cream

1 egg, beaten

Steps

1. Pre-heat your oven to 425°F. Line the bottom of an 8-inch round cake pan with parchment paper.

2. In a large bowl, whisk the cornmeal, flour, sugar, baking powder, baking soda, and salt.

3. In a medium bowl, whisk the sour cream, green onions, jalapeño peppers, Cumin Oil, heavy cream, and egg until smooth.

4. Fold the sour cream mixture into the cornmeal mixture, just until it is combined.

5. Spoon the mixture into the prepared cake pan and even the top out.

6. Place into the oven and bake 30 minutes.

7. Remove from the oven and let cool in the pan 10 minutes.

8. Remove the High Desert Cornbread from the pan and let cool on a wire rack.

Homemade Flour Tortillas

(Makes varying amounts, depending on tortilla size)

You cannot be serious about Southwest cooking if you cannot make a flour tortilla at home; it really is that simple. Speaking of simple, just look at the ingredients for Homemade Flour Tortillas. Homemade Flour Tortillas are just downright delicious, and that is even before you use them with anything else. If you have ever had a freshly made tortilla, you know that this simple combination of flour, salt, lard, and water is delicious. Matter of fact, it is habit-forming, and no, they do not taste anything like the generic flour tortillas you find at your market.

The most important thing to remember when making flour tortillas is the fact that you are not a machine. What do I mean? Your tortillas will not be perfectly round nor will each one of them be the exact same thickness. Do not worry about this; it isn't important. You are eating them, not marveling at them. As time goes by and you work out all the little idiosyncrasies of making flour tortillas, your tortillas will look just like the ones at the old-fashioned tortilla houses which used to dot the Southwest.

Now we come to cooking the tortillas. Any type of pan or griddle will work fine. You can even use a grill or grill pan. The most important thing to remember: use no oil on the pan or on the grill. The tortilla dough has lard (rendered animal fat) in it, and when the tortilla is being cooked, the lard will naturally keep it from sticking. As opposed to their chemically induced, mass-produced counterparts, Homemade Flour Tortillas do not freeze well. Use them the same day you make them, and if you should have any left over, keep them in a zip-lock bag in the fridge for a day or two.

Ingredients
¼ cup lard
3 cups flour
2 tsp. salt
1 cup boiling water

Steps
1. In a medium bowl, combine the lard and flour and, using your fingers (or a pastry blender), rub the lard into the flour until the mixture is crumbly.
2. Stir in the salt and water to form a dough.
3. Place the dough onto a floured surface and knead 5 minutes. Yes, the dough will be hot, so be careful.
4. Cover the dough with a lint-free towel or bowl and let it rest 20 minutes.

5. Remove portions of the dough (size depends on how big you want the tortilla to be). Place them on a floured surface and roll them out to about ½-inch thickness (depending on how you will be using them).

6. Heat a pan or griddle over medium heat. Do not add any oil to the pan.

7. Place the tortillas in the pan (in batches) and cook just until they begin to blister (bubbles appear). Turn over and cook 1 minute longer.

8. Remove the tortillas and keep them between pieces of waxed paper (or parchment paper) until ready to use.

Mexican Dried Shrimp Fried Dumplings

(Serving amount depends on size)

I guess if you really wanted to stretch things, you can say that Mexican Dried Shrimp Fried Dumplings are the Southwest way of making Southern hushpuppies. They are quite similar in preparation, but when it comes to taste and texture, there are vast differences. How you serve these little delights of yumminess strictly depends on you. They can be served as you would cornbread or tortillas. You can also serve them with a myriad of sauces. Yes, they are very versatile, as are most dishes in the Southwest kitchen.

What are dried shrimp? Well . . . they are shrimp which have been dehydrated. You can find dried shrimp in many Latino markets and most Asian markets. Supermarkets with a good ethnic food section will also usually have them in stock. They are little shrimp, about the size of bay or salad shrimp, and sold in packages. They are a little costly, but they hold a lot of flavor. One small package is about all you need to make Mexican Dried Shrimp Fried Dumplings.

The reason you are using just the egg white in this dish and not the whole egg is for the texture of the dumpling. These are much lighter than you might expect. If you were to use the egg yolk as well, the fried dumpling would be denser. The egg white used will not only lighten the batter but will act as an adhering factor for the ingredients. It's Kitchen Science 101.

Ingredients

1 cup flour
1 cup cold water
¼ tsp. salt
¾ cup dried shrimp
1 egg white
½ white onion, peeled and minced
5 serrano peppers, minced
peanut oil or vegetable oil for frying

Steps

1. In a medium bowl, whisk the flour, water, and salt and set aside.
2. Place the dried shrimp into a bowl of hot water and let soak for 10 minutes. Drain the shrimp and discard the liquid.

3. In a small bowl, whisk the egg white to form stiff peaks.

4. Add the egg white, shrimp, onion, and peppers to the flour mixture and stir just until blended.

5. In a large sauté pan or skillet, heat ½ inch oil to 325°F on a deep-fry thermometer.

6. Spoon some batter into the pan and fry until golden on both sides.

7. Remove the dumpling with a slotted spoon and place on a paper towel–lined plate to soak up any excess oil.

8. Let cool slightly before serving.

Olive Oil Bread

(Makes 2 loaves)

It is a simple fact of food. Italians will say their olive oil is the best. The Mediterranean people will say their olive oil is the best. Spain will say their olive oil is the best. Any place that makes their own olive oil will say theirs is the best. Well, they may all be right in one way or the other, but the simple fact is that the olive oils made in the great American Southwest are the tastiest and most vibrant, and yes, I am prejudiced in this matter.

Any country or region known for its olive oil has their version of Olive Oil Bread, and they are all quite delicious. The great thing about a bread of this type is that it will take on the subtleties of each of the various olive oils used. If you use a Southwest olive oil, you will have a full-bodied flavor and a little richer color due to the types of olives grown in the Southwest. Olive Oil Bread, no matter what kind, is a perfect dinner table bread as it will not clash with any other dish. Personally, this is one of my favorite breads to serve with any kind of soup.

If you are a breadmaker, you will find the dough for this bread to be rather interesting. It is a sticky (wet) dough and can be a little messy during the first kneading. I think you will find it much more advantageous to do the initial kneading of this dough within the bowl. By the second kneading, the dough will be soft, but you can knead it by hand.

Ingredients

2 tsp. yeast
2 cups warm water, divided
¼ tsp. sugar
4¾ cups flour, divided
2 tsp. salt
¼ cup olive oil

Steps

1. In a large bowl, whisk the yeast, ¼ cup warm water, and sugar. Set the bowl aside 10 minutes for the yeast to proof (foam).

2. Into the yeast, stir 2 cups flour and ¾ cup warm water to form a soft dough.

3. Knead the bread, in the bowl, for 10 minutes. It will be rather sticky.

4. Add the remaining flour, the remaining warm water, salt, and olive oil.

5. Place the dough on a floured surface and knead 10 minutes. It will be sticky at first but turn soft as it gets kneaded.

6. Divide the dough in half.

7. Line two baking sheets with parchment paper or a silicone baking sheet.

8. With floured hands, form each half of dough into a round loaf.

9. Place one loaf on each prepared baking sheet and let rise 1 hour.

10. Pre-heat your oven to 375°F.

11. Place the loaves into the oven (put each baking sheet on its own rack, one above the other) and bake 50 minutes, exchanging racks halfway through for even baking.

12. Remove the breads from the oven and let cool on a wire rack.

··· Note ···

For a little richer flavor and look: once the bread comes out of the oven, brush it with some extra olive oil.

Pita Bread

(Makes varying amounts, depending on size)

Pita Bread, also known as "pocket bread" is not native to the American Southwest. It is actually native to the Near East and can date back to 2500 BC Mesopotamia. Yeah, it's been around for a while. Where it comes into play with Southwest cuisine is the fact that it is one of our favorite sandwich breads. You bake some fresh Pita Bread and then fill the pockets with the flavors of the Southwest. Of course, it also helps that it is a fast (not including rising time) and easy bread to make because, let's face it, when you're hungry, you want food now!

Pita Bread is a fun bread to make, but to make it properly requires very intense heat. This intense heat is what creates the pocket. When you put the bread into the oven, the intense heat creates an internal steam within the dough, and what happens is the two layers of dough internally separate. Once the bread is removed from the oven and it cools down, the separation creates the pocket. You may also notice the very short baking time. This is not a misprint—it really only takes about 6 minutes total to bake Pita Bread (depending on the size).

Now to the question of whether Pita Bread should be baked on a stone or on tiles or simply on a baking sheet. True Pita Bread should always be baked on a stone or clay tiles, and in this case, it is of the utmost importance to make sure the stone or tiles are properly pre-heated (it takes a while to pre-heat a baking stone). Most people do not have a baking stone or baking tiles; in those cases, yes, you can use a baking sheet, but unlike with most breads or baked products, while you are pre-heating the oven, you will want to also pre-heat the baking sheet. This initial heat is of great importance in the Pita Bread turning out properly.

Ingredients
2½ tsp. yeast
½ cup warm water
1 Tbs. honey
3 cups flour
1 tsp. salt
1 cup cold water

Steps
1. In a small bowl, whisk the yeast, warm water, and honey. Set the bowl aside 10 minutes for the yeast to proof (foam).

2. In a large bowl, stir the proofed yeast, flour, salt, and cold water to form a dough.

3. Place the dough onto a floured surface and knead 10 minutes.

4. Place the dough back into the bowl, cover, and let rise 2 hours.

5. Pre-heat your oven to 500°F (if your oven can go to 525°F or 550°F, that is fine too). Make sure the rack is as close to the bottom of the oven as possible.

6. Place the dough onto a floured surface and knead 5 minutes.

7. Remove portions of the dough and roll out into a circle of ¼-inch thickness (size depends on your preference).

8. Let the pieces of dough rest 15 minutes.

9. Place the breads onto the hot baking sheet or stones in the oven.

10. Bake the bread for 4 minutes.

11. Turn the breads over and bake 2 minutes.

12. Remove the breads from the oven and let cool before using.

··· Note ···
The bread must cool before the pocket can be formed.

Puff Bread

(Makes 14 pieces)

I am sure that, sometime during your life, you have heard the adage "cooking can be fun." This adage is very true—you can have a lot of fun in the kitchen—and what is even better is that you can eat the fun you've made. You, however, never hear anyone say that breadmaking can be fun. Well, I am here to prove breadmaking can be fun, and Puff Bread is a perfect example. I guess the best way to describe Puff Bread is to say that you are going to be making bread balloons!

If you have never eaten Puff Bread before, you are missing out. Not only is it quite tasty, you can do so much with it. As its name implies, it is a puffed bread. When you break the bread apart (you never cut Puff Bread, you only rip it apart), you will have two hollow pieces of bread. Into the hollowed crevice, you can place anything from savory to sweet. If you make them big enough, you can even use them as edible bowls for salsas on your festive party table. See, I told you they were fun!

You will find a rather strange ingredient in this dish as far as breads are concerned. Into this dough, you are going to be adding yogurt (plain, not flavored). What this does is twofold: First, it will give the bread a nice flavor, and second, it is basically what congeals the dough and makes it balloon. This is a deep-fried bread, so temperature is very important to the bread puffing up. Make sure you have a deep-fry thermometer. As far as what oil to use, peanut oil would be best due to the intense heat, but a canola or vegetable oil will work fine too.

Ingredients
3 cups flour
1 tsp. salt
1 Tbs. sugar
1 tsp. baking powder
1 tsp. ground cumin
2 Tbs. melted butter
⅔ cup plain yogurt
½ cup water
peanut oil for frying

Steps
1. In a large bowl, whisk the flour, salt, sugar, baking powder, and cumin.
2. Stir in the butter, yogurt, and water to form a dough.

3. Remove the dough to a floured surface and knead 10 minutes.

4. Place a lint-free towel or bowl over the dough and let it rest 10 minutes.

5. In a large, deep sauté pan or skillet, heat 3 inches of oil to 350°F on a deep-fry thermometer.

6. Divide the dough into 14 portions and form each into a 2-inch round of about ¼-inch thickness.

7. Carefully place the dough portions into the hot oil (in batches) and fry until they puff up and turn golden in color.

8. Using a slotted spoon, remove the bread to a paper towel–lined plate to soak up any excess oil.

9. Let the bread cool before using.

Real Garlic Bread

(Makes 12 rolls/buns)

Garlic bread. What is it? To answer that question honestly, let us first look at what garlic bread is not. It is not a piece of any type of bread slathered with an industrial gunk with fake garlic flavoring that many restaurants serve. It is not yesterday's soon-to-be-stale bread with butter spread upon it and then seasoned with garlic salt. Real Garlic Bread is an artisanal bread made with garlic . . . real garlic. It is a bread made to be cherished.

This is how I make garlic bread in the Southwest. I don't play games. When I say it is garlic bread, it is garlic bread—and this has ten cloves of garlic in it! You might think this is overkill. It is not. When garlic is baked into a dish, such as this bread, you will only be tasting the essential oils of the garlic as the pulp itself will pretty much disintegrate. Yes, you will taste the garlic—that is the whole idea of the bread—but you won't be bowled over by it. Of course, you can always use less garlic if you desire (or more if you're having a problem with vampires).

This is a yeast bread, so it does take some time to make as, with most yeast breads, you will have a few rising periods. On the subject of yeast, whenever I call for yeast, I am referring to the active dry yeast you buy at the market. Nothing fancy nor the caked yeast you find in the refrigerated section of some markets. Just simple, everyday, regular yeast.

Ingredients

4½ cups flour
¼ cup sugar
2 tsp. yeast
1¾ cups warm water
10 cloves garlic, peeled and minced
1 Tbs. olive oil

Steps

1. In a large bowl, stir the flour, sugar, yeast, and water to form a dough.
2. Place the dough onto a floured surface and knead 5 minutes.
3. Place the dough back into the bowl, cover, and let rise 1 hour.
4. Place the dough on a floured surface and knead 5 minutes.
5. Place back into the bowl, cover again, and let rise 1 more hour.
6. In a small bowl, combine the garlic and oil to form a paste-like consistency.

7. Place the dough onto a floured surface and divide into 12 portions.

8. Flatten each portion with your hands.

9. Place some of the garlic paste into the middle of the dough and then roll the dough into a ball.

10. Line two baking sheet with parchment paper or a silicone baking sheet.

11. Place the dough onto the prepared baking sheet and let rise 30 minutes.

12. Preheat your oven to 400°F.

13. Place into the oven and bake 20 minutes.

14. Remove the breads from the oven and let cool on a wire rack.

Sour Cream Whole Wheat Bread

(Makes 2 loaves)

Every nutritional study that you read says you should eat whole wheat bread. No one can argue with these studies (unless of course you have gluten problems), but here is something you might not have known. In the United States, most of the breads labeled as "wheat bread" are in fact white bread with molasses to darken the bread into looking like whole wheat bread. How do they get away with this, and is it legal? Yes, it is legal, and the reason is that the bread is indeed made with wheat flour (same as white bread). For nutritional purposes, you only want bread that is labeled as "whole wheat bread" and not "wheat bread."

Sour Cream Whole Wheat Bread is, as its title suggests, a whole wheat bread. The best thing about this whole wheat bread is not just its angelic texture but the fresh flavor of the bread, thanks to the inclusion of the sour cream. The sour cream adds to its richness and gives it just a tad of acidity, which turns the loaves into something truly special. Once your friends and family taste this bread, they will think you have gone to the finest bakery in your town. Did I mention this is also one of the easiest and simplest breads you will ever make at home?

As with any whole wheat bread, you will also be using a typical white flour. Why? Whole wheat flour is very heavy, and if you did use it, the bread wouldn't rise as much and the texture of the bread would be very dense. When you go to your market to buy whole wheat flour, check the label on the package carefully as you want it to say "stone ground wheat." As for the white flour here, any all-purpose white flour will be fine. No need to waste money on the so-called "bread flour" for this Sour Cream Whole Wheat Bread.

Ingredients

1 Tbs. yeast
½ cup warm water
2 tsp. raw honey
½ cup milk
1 cup sour cream
1 Tbs. sugar
1½ tsp. salt
1 Tbs. melted butter
1¾ cups whole wheat flour
1¾ cups white or all-purpose flour

Steps

1. In a large bowl, whisk the yeast, water, and honey. Set the bowl aside 10 minutes for the yeast to proof (foam).

2. Into the proofed yeast, whisk the milk, sour cream, sugar, salt, and butter.

3. Stir in the whole wheat flour and white flour to form a dough.

4. Place the dough on a floured surface and knead 5 minutes.

5. Place the dough back into the bowl, cover, and let rise 2 hours.

6. Punch the dough down and divide in half.

7. Line a baking sheet with parchment paper or a silicone baking sheet.

8. Form each half of the dough into a long loaf.

9. Place the loaves onto the prepared baking sheet and let rise 1 hour.

10. Pre-heat your oven to 400°F.

11. Place the loaves into the oven and bake 35 minutes.

12. Remove the breads from the oven and let cool on a wire rack.

Apple Upside-Down Tequila Cake

(Makes 1 cake)

In the South, they take a lot of pride in their famed peach upside-down cake, and they should—it is scrumptious. Here in the great American Southwest, we too have an upside-down cake, and we take a lot of pride in ours as it combines two food elements which were made for each other: apples and tequila! The combination of apples and liquor has been a favorite for many centuries, and to prove this fact, just look at the liqueurs which combine the two. They create a fascinating flavor combination, but it does depend on the variety of apple you pair the liquor with.

For Apple Upside-Down Tequila Cake, we use a Granny Smith apple. You can find these in all markets year-round. They are a smaller green apple with a slightly tart flavor and a crunchy vibrant texture. They are great for baking because their fibers do not break down as easy as other apple varieties, and their flavor is accentuated by the use of the tequila. Though this is a perfect dessert for any holiday table, I also like to serve this during outdoor parties when the main courses feature grilled or barbecued entrees.

Apple Upside-Down Tequila Cake is made in a typical cake pan, and yes, if you're from the South, you can use a cast iron skillet. You do want to sauté the apples before making the cake, and this is for two reasons: First, you want to soften the apples, and secondly, you want to blend all the flavors with the natural apple juice which comes from sautéing them. If you have never made an upside-down cake, the bottom of the cake will be the top when it is presented. To remove it from the pan, just invert (turn over) the pan onto a plate bigger than the pan. Quite simple!

Ingredients

2 Granny Smith apples, peeled, cored, and thinly sliced
⅓ cup brown sugar, divided
¼ cup tequila
¼ cup butter
2 egg yolks, beaten
⅓ cup sour cream
1 cup flour
½ cup sugar
½ tsp. baking powder
¼ tsp. salt
6 Tbs. shortening

Steps

1. In a large bowl, toss the apples with 2 tablespoons of brown sugar and the tequila. Set the bowl aside for 30 minutes so the apples can macerate (soak).

2. Pre-heat your oven to 350°F. Line the bottom of an 8-inch round cake pan with parchment paper.

3. In a medium sauté pan, melt the butter over medium heat. Stir in the remaining brown sugar until it has dissolved.

4. Place the apples and their marinade into the pan, bring the mixture to a boil, and cook until most of the liquid has evaporated (you will have a lovely syrup).

5. Place the apples into the bottom of the prepared cake pan and pour the sauce atop.

6. In a mixer with the paddle attachment, beat the egg yolks, sour cream, flour, sugar, baking powder, salt, and shortening until you have a batter.

7. Spoon the batter over the apples and spread to even out.

8. Place into the oven and bake 40 minutes.

9. Remove the cake from the oven and let cool in the pan 5 minutes.

10. Invert the pan onto a serving plate and let cool before serving.

Applewood Smoked Bacon Ice Cream

(Makes about 4 cups)

Even before the bacon craze in food, here in the Southwest, we have used this smoked pork belly in many of our dishes. Just as the bacon craze was starting to bloom, Casa de Cuisine introduced a bacon ice cream. Yes, we were the first to do this, and this fact can be quantified via an Internet search. Since then, many others have adapted our recipe, and this is always a compliment. At first, people sort of squinched their faces at the thought of a bacon ice cream, but once they tasted it, they were hooked. By the way, we created Applewood Smoked Bacon Ice Cream by accident!

There is a very simple secret to our Applewood Smoked Bacon Ice Cream, and for the very first time, I will share that secret. When you cook the bacon for this ice cream, you will have the rendered bacon fat. You want to be sure to add that fat to the ice cream as it will not only make for a smooth, rich texture, it will add an immense amount of flavor. Don't worry about the fat intake here—this is ice cream; it is supposed to be fattening!

The sweetening aspect of this ice cream is very natural. We use no sugar. The only sweetness is pure maple syrup. This is important! Do not use that stuff they call "maple pancake syrup." There is no maple in that stuff. It is an artificially colored and flavored corn syrup, and it's terrible for you. Only use pure maple syrup. Yes, it is rather expensive, but this is something you're putting into your body. If you're wondering why we add glazed pecans to this ice cream, well . . . I just like glazed pecans! If you don't share my affection, simply leave them out.

Ingredients

2 cups heavy cream

1 cup milk

¾ cup pure maple syrup

½ cup cooked bacon, minced, plus the rendered fat

¼ tsp. salt

½ tsp. ground nutmeg

½ cup chopped glazed pecans

Steps

1. In a large bowl, whisk the heavy cream, milk, maple syrup, bacon, bacon fat, salt, and nutmeg.
2. Place the bowl in the refrigerator and chill at least 2 hours.
3. Pour the mixture into an ice cream machine and follow the manufacturer's instructions.
4. Once the ice cream gets to the soft-serve texture, add the glazed pecans.
5. Freeze until ready to serve.

Blackberry Cranberry Pie

(Makes 1 pie)

Pie! Everyone loves a freshly baked pie, and fruit pies are among the all-time favorites. Matter of fact, to eat pie is to be American if one were to believe the adage "as American as apple pie." Mind you, to be factual, apple pie is originally a French dessert, but let's not be nitpicky. No matter what the season may be, anytime is the perfect time for pie.

It is a pretty safe bet that, if you were to walk anywhere in the great American Southwest, somewhere along your travels you will saunter upon a blackberry bush. It may be on a trail, in a garden, or on a highway. We have a ton of wonderful, naturally sweet blackberries growing everywhere. Look into any Southwest kitchen, and there is a good chance you'll see blackberry preserves, pickled blackberries, bags of frozen blackberries, and of course blackberry juice stains on the counters. Because of our insatiable love of blackberries, blackberry pie is one of our favorites, and when you combine blackberries with dried cranberries, your mouth is in for something special.

An important part of any pie is the pie crust. Later on in this section, I will share with you the only Pie Crust I ever use (page 230). It is a very simple recipe and very classic. The reason it is the only pie crust I use is because it is perfect for either fruit pies or cream pies. On the subject of crust, this Blackberry Cranberry Pie does not have a top crust to it. Instead, we are going to top it with a streusel-type crust, and we're going to do it Southwest style!

Ingredients
prepared Pie Crust (page 230)

For Streusel Topping
2 cups rolled oats (oatmeal)
½ cup butter, softened
½ cup brown sugar
½ cup chopped walnuts
1 Tbs. vanilla

For Pie Filling
2 cups fresh blackberries
1 cup dried cranberries
½ cup sugar
¼ cup Southwest Style Crème Fraîche (page 17)

Steps

1. To make the streusel topping: In a medium bowl, combine all of the ingredients until crumbly. Cover the bowl and set aside until ready to use.

2. In a large bowl, combine the blackberries, cranberries, and sugar. Let the mixture sit 10 minutes.

3. Stir the Southwest Style Crème Fraîche into the berries.

4. Spoon the filling into the prepared Pie Crust.

5. Place into the oven and bake 20 minutes.

6. Sprinkle the streusel topping over the pie and bake an additional 20 minutes.

7. Remove the pie from the oven and let cool before serving.

Blackberry Frozen Custard

(Makes about 5 cups)

Whether it be ice creams, sorbets, gelatos, or frozen custards, we all seem to love frozen desserts. One of the reasons for this is that they are refreshing, but the refreshing aspects go beyond taste. They actually refresh our mouth and tongue—especially here in the Southwest since we use a lot of seasonings. In many cases, these frozen desserts also help our internal organs during the course of digesting what we have just eaten. So, yes, in a roundabout way, frozen desserts are indeed good for you.

Perhaps you have never enjoyed a scoop of frozen custard. It is not really as known in many parts of the world as ice cream, so you might be wondering what it actually is. Well, it is actually a frozen custard! It is like an ice cream base, yet it is cooked before churning and features egg yolks and heavy cream. Yes, it is rather decadent, and yes, it has a lot of calories. It is also very simple to make at home, and since you only live once, enjoy it! The plain simple syrup this recipe calls for you can make at home; just see the note below.

For this Blackberry Frozen Custard, we are going to make a natural blackberry syrup, and it is very simple as the recipe steps will show you. When making a syrup of this type, you can either strain it through a fine sieve or not—the choice in yours. If strained, you will remove all the little seeds, but some people like the texture of the seeds. You are going to strain the custard through a fine sieve. The reason for this is to make sure no cooked (scrambled) portions of eggs are in the final product. Once you get used to making a custard mixture like this, the straining can be eliminated as you will know by look and feel when the mixture is perfectly cooked.

Ingredients

2 cups blackberries
1 cup simple syrup (see note)
2 cups milk
2 cups heavy cream
1 cup sugar
¼ tsp. salt
1 Tbs. vanilla
5 egg yolks

Steps

1. Into a food processor, add the blackberries and simple syrup and puree.

2. Strain the puree through a fine sieve and chill until ready to use.

3. In a medium saucepan, whisk the milk, heavy cream, sugar, salt, and vanilla over medium heat. Cook until it just comes to a simmer. Do not let it boil.

4. In a medium bowl, whisk the egg yolks.

5. Whisk 1 cup of the hot cream mixture into the egg yolks.

6. Slowly whisk the egg yolk mixture into the rest of the hot cream in the saucepan and cook, while stirring, until it has thickened.

7. Strain the custard through a fine sieve to remove any cooked portions of egg.

8. Chill the custard mixture at least 2 hours.

9. Stir the blackberry syrup into the custard mixture.

10. Pour the mixture into an ice cream machine and follow the manufacturer's instructions.

11. Freeze the Blackberry Frozen Custard until ready to serve.

··· Note ···

To make your own simple syrup: Combine equal parts sugar and water in a pot, heat over medium heat, and stir until the sugar dissolves and the water is clear. That's it! Keep the simple syrup in a bottle and either refrigerate it or, if you're going to be using it often, put it in your pantry.

Buttermilk Frozen Custard

(Makes about 5 cups)

If you have ever tasted buttermilk on its own, you are very well aware of the fact that it is nasty! It is wonderful in baked products like biscuits (see Buttermilk Biscuits on page 190), it is great when soaking chicken for fried chicken, and it is great in certain sauces—but on its own, it is nasty! With that noted, you might be hesitant to try a frozen custard using buttermilk. I was, and then when the first satiny smooth spoonful hit my tongue, I was enthralled.

Elsewhere in this section, I go into frozen custards with the recipe for Blackberry Frozen Custard (page 220), but for this Buttermilk Frozen Custard, there are a few differences, aside from the buttermilk. Into the mixture, we are going to add almond extract, and this is going to temper the acidity of the buttermilk and give this dessert a wonderful aroma.

As you will note from the ingredients, this Buttermilk Frozen Custard is indeed a dieter's worst nightmare. This is okay. It is a dessert really made for special occasions, like any day that ends with a "y." Due to the acidity in the buttermilk, this is actually a great dessert to serve after a spicy grilled or barbecued dinner as the buttermilk will help cleanse the tongue and the frozen custard will help refresh the mouth.

Ingredients

2 cups heavy cream
1 cup sugar
¼ tsp. salt
1 cup buttermilk
½ tsp. almond extract
6 egg yolks

Steps

1. In a medium saucepan over medium heat, whisk the heavy cream, sugar, salt, buttermilk, and almond extract until the sugar has dissolved.

2. In a medium bowl, whisk the egg yolks.

3. Whisk 1 cup of the hot cream into the egg yolks.

4. Slowly whisk the egg yolks into the rest of the hot cream in the saucepan and then stir until the mixture thickens. Do not let it come to a boil.

5. Strain the custard mixture through a fine sieve to remove any cooked portions of eggs.

6. Let the custard cool to room temperature.

7. Chill the custard at least 2 hours.

8. Pour the custard into an ice cream machine and follow the manufacturer's instructions.

9. Freeze the Buttermilk Frozen Custard until ready to serve.

Buttermilk Pie

(Makes 1 pie)

Maybe this is a generational thing, but for many people, a cream pie is a comfort food. It might have to do with the fact that, for many of us who were raised in a lower to middle-income family, a cream pie was the most inexpensive pie to be made (or bought at the market). If the cream pie was of the fruit-flavored variety, it was a way for our moms (or whoever did the cooking) to use up fruit before it spoiled. In the kitchens of yesteryear (and in today's Southwest kitchen), nothing goes to waste.

Buttermilk Pie is a staple of the typical Southern kitchen and was brought to the Southwest during the national migration from the South to the West. Since buttermilk (a cultured milk) lasted longer than regular milk (which at the time was not pasteurized), this pie became a popular dessert for Sunday suppers. It is a very simple pie to make and almost impossible to mess up!

As with most of the pies I make, I always use the same crust, and you can find that recipe on page 230. This pie only uses a bottom crust, so there is no need to contemplate any type of topping. What will happen, however, is the top of the cream mixture will get a nice light caramelization. Not only does this look good, it gives it a little more flavor. Here in the Southwest we have made a little adaption to the original Southern Buttermilk Pie with a dash of grated nutmeg and some grated lemon zest.

Ingredients

prepared Pie Crust (page 230)
¼ cup butter, softened
2 cups sugar
3 eggs, beaten
⅓ cup flour
1 cup buttermilk
1 tsp. finely grated lemon zest
⅛ tsp. ground nutmeg

Steps

1. Pre-heat your oven to 350°F.

2. In a mixer with the paddle attachment, beat the butter, sugar, and eggs until smooth and creamy.

3. Add the flour and beat 5 minutes (remember to scrape down the bowl a few times).

4. Add the buttermilk, lemon zest, and nutmeg and beat 5 minutes. This length of time is important for the proper emulsifying of the buttermilk.

5. Pour into the unbaked pie crust.

6. Place into the oven and bake 60 minutes.

7. Remove the pie from the oven and let cool to room temperature.

8. Chill the pie before serving.

Cactus Pear Sorbet

(Makes about 2 cups)

You may have seen these strange little fruits in your supermarket produce section and wondered "what are they?" These look like something from prehistoric times with their little needles and/or bumps protruding from their skin, but just wait until you slice one open. You will see a brilliant magenta color dotted with a multitude of seeds. These are cactus pears, or as they are sometimes referred to, prickly pears. And yes, they are a fruit which indeed does grow on a cactus—to be more precise, the Opuntia cactus.

Though you can peel a cactus pear and eat it, you would be doing a lot of spitting since these little guys are loaded with seeds. The best way to use them is to make a syrup, and when you make that syrup, you can make a quintessential Southwest frozen dessert called Cactus Pear Sorbet. It is hard to describe the flavor of the cactus pear other than to note it is extremely fresh tasting. It isn't very sweet, and that is why we will be adding some plain simple syrup to it. Also, when dealing with any frozen dessert, the sweet taste is usually a little weak to the tongue, thus most frozen desserts have what may look like too much sugar.

Ingredients

8–10 cactus pears (depending on their size), peeled and chopped
2 cups simple syrup (see note)
1 tsp. finely grated lemon zest
1 Tbs. lemon juice
¼ tsp. salt

Steps

1. Place the cactus pears into a food processor and puree.
2. Strain the puree through a fine sieve and discard the seeds.
3. In a large bowl, whisk the cactus pear puree, simple syrup, lemon zest, lemon juice, and salt.
4. Place the mixture into the refrigerator and chill at least 2 hours.
5. Pour the mixture into an ice cream machine and follow the manufacturer's instructions.
6. Freeze until ready to serve.

Frozen Kahlúa Custard

(Makes about 4 cups)

You may have noticed throughout this book, we here in the Southwest do indeed love our Kahlúa. Whether it be used in a drink, a sauce, a side dish or an entrée—we love Kahlúa. Of course, part of our fondness comes from the fact that it is a Southwest original (factually Mexico) but also because its natural flavoring goes with pretty much everything in the Southwest kitchen, including this incredible frozen dessert called Frozen Kahlúa Custard.

Now, you might be thinking, "Hey, wait a minute, I thought alcohol doesn't freeze?" Your assumption is correct . . . in most cases. Due to the fact that Kahlúa has a very low percentage of alcohol, it will not freeze solid, but it will get "slushy." This "slushiness" will be enveloped by its frozen surroundings, and the molecules will indeed solidify. Cooking is science!

I must tell you we have tried to make a "lite" version of our frozen custards by replacing the heavy cream with half-and-half. They have all been rather tasty, but when it comes to the texture and richness of the dessert, they have also been dismal failures. I would not recommend making any changes to the recipes and since frozen custards are not a daily dessert (for many), remember the words of Julia Child who always used the word "moderation" when talking about high-fat foods.

Ingredients

1 cup milk
2½ cups heavy cream
1 cup sugar, divided
5 egg yolks
1 Tbs. vanilla
¼ tsp. salt
1 cup Kahlúa

Steps

1. In a medium saucepan over medium heat, whisk the milk, heavy cream, and ½ cup sugar until the sugar dissolves and it just comes to a simmer. Do not let it boil.

2. In a medium bowl, whisk the egg yolks, remaining sugar, vanilla, and salt.

3. Whisk 1 cup of the hot cream into the egg mixture.

4. Slowly whisk the egg mixture into the remaining hot cream in the saucepan and then stir until it becomes thickened.

5. Strain the custard through a fine sieve to remove any cooked (scrambled) egg.

6. Let the custard cool to room temperature and then chill at least 2 hours.

7. Once the mixture has chilled, stir in the Kahlúa.

8. Pour the mixture into an ice cream machine and follow the manufacturer's instructions.

9. Place into the freezer until ready to serve.

··· Note ···

Since this ice cream does contain alcohol, you may need to freeze it a little longer once it has churned.

Pie Crust

(Makes 1 bottom or top crust for an 8–10-inch pie)

There are many bakers and pastry chefs who will tell you in no uncertain terms that a pie is only as good as its crust. I fully concur with this, and it is for this reason that this pie crust is the only one I use for all my fruit pies and most of my cream pies. It is a very simple crust to make, and for you gourmands, it is also the most famous French pie crust in the world. I call it a simple pie crust, but gourmands call it pâte brisée.

There is only one important element you must remember when making this pie crust (or any pastry featuring butter). You want to use only a top quality sweet butter. Yes, this makes all the difference in the world. When it comes to the flour, just use an unbleached all-purpose flour. No need to waste money on some fancy flour. You can make this in a food processor (which I would never do), or you can buy a nifty little gadget called a "pastry blender." They only cost a few bucks, and chances are, this is what your mother or grandmother used to make her pie crusts.

Don't be concerned if your pie crust does not come out perfect the first few times. It does take a while to get used to the feel of the crust. It will taste perfect, and once you've done it a few times, it will look perfect. Because this is a butter crust, once you have made the dough, make sure you chill it for about 15 minutes before you roll it out. You can make this ahead of time and keep it chilled between sheets of plastic wrap or waxed paper. This recipe, as noted above, will make one top or bottom crust for a pie of 8 to 10 inches in diameter.

Ingredients
1¼ cup flour
2 tsp. sugar
½ tsp. salt
½ cup butter, chilled and diced
3 Tbs. ice water

Steps
1. In a large bowl, whisk the flour, sugar, and salt.
2. Using a pastry blender, cut the butter into the flour until you have a crumbly mixture. This can also be done in a food processor.

3. Gradually stir in the ice water, a ½ tablespoon at a time, to make a dough. (Adding the water at a slow pace is important as the humidity in your kitchen at any given time may affect the moisture of your dough. You may find that you don't need all of the ice water, or perhaps you need a little bit more than called for.)

4. Place the dough on a floured surface and knead just enough to bring the dough together, about a minute or two.

5. Wrap the dough in plastic wrap and chill 15 minutes. The dough needs to be chilled to solidify the butter again. This not only makes the rolling of the crust easier, it also gives it a more flakey texture. (If your pie recipe calls for an unbaked pie crust, then just skip the next few baking steps and follow the recipe for the pie it will be used for.)

6. Pre-heat your oven to 375°F.

7. Place the dough on a floured surface and roll out to fit your pie plate/pan.

8. Place the crust into the pie plate/pan and prick all over with the tines of a fork.

9. Place into the oven and bake 25–30 minutes.

10. Remove from the oven and let cool completely before filling the crust.

Pure Honey Frozen Vanilla Custard

(Makes about 5 cups)

Honey, in its pure and raw form, is one of the greatest gifts Mother Nature has bestowed upon us. There are currently numerous scientific and medical studies centering on the health aspects of honey and all of them, as of this writing, are proving one thing: honey is a super food, and its effect on numerous illnesses and diseases is beyond reproach. Sadly, however, as of this writing, we seem to be losing our battle to save the honey bees. The simple fact is, without bees, we will all perish. Here is an interesting honey fact: in the course of its short lifespan, one honey bee will only yield ½ teaspoon of honey.

On the subject of honey, most of the honey sold in supermarkets is not real. You can basically call anything "honey," but you cannot call it "pure" and "raw" unless it actually is—and this also means it is unpasteurized. Yes, pure and raw honey does cost more, but the benefits are amazing, not to mention the taste. Raw honey will crystalize, but this is no problem—just heat it for a bit. Raw and pure honey will never go bad, and as a matter of fact, the raw honey buried with King Tut is still good!

There has always been a great debate about ice cream and how it should be served. Should it be hard or sort of soft? From a flavor standpoint, ice cream should always be served at a soft stage or as soft-serve. The colder and more frozen a food, the less flavor. If your ice cream gets too hard, simply leave it out of the freezer for about 10 minutes. Usually—and this depends on the ingredients—it should be perfect right from the ice cream machine.

Ingredients

2 cups milk
2 cups heavy cream
2 cups raw honey
2 Tbs. vanilla
¼ tsp. salt
½ tsp. ground nutmeg
5 egg yolks

Steps

1. In a medium saucepan over medium heat, whisk the milk, heavy cream, honey, vanilla, salt, and nutmeg and bring to a simmer. Do not let it come to a boil.

2. In a medium bowl, whisk the egg yolks with 1 cup of the hot cream.

3. Slowly whisk the egg mixture into the remaining hot cream in the saucepan and then stir the mixture until it thickens.

4. Strain the custard through a fine sieve to remove any cooked egg.

5. Cool the custard to room temperature.

6. Chill the custard at least 2 hours.

7. Pour the custard into an ice cream machine and follow the manufacturer's instructions.

8. Freeze the Pure Honey Frozen Vanilla Custard until ready to serve.

Spiced Bananas with Kahlúa and Rum

(Serves 4)

Bananas are one of the most popular foods in the world. They are grown in one hundred seventy countries on this globe we call Earth. They are seventy-five percent water, and as opposed to popular belief, they are relatively low in potassium, and if you have a latex allergy, bananas can cause a reaction. Also of note, botanically speaking, bananas are a berry, and the banana plant is the largest flowering herb on earth. See, food can be fun!

Personally speaking, I don't think there is anything worse to put into your mouth, from a texture point of view, than a cooked banana . . . but when it comes to a "raw" version of a dessert featuring bananas, I think they are incredible. With this dessert, we don't cook or heat the bananas; instead, we cook the sauce to be put onto the bananas. You will get the full flavor and texture of the bananas and a dessert which is nothing short of memorable.

As you might surmise from the title of this dessert, there is alcohol involved, and it appears in the sauce. There are those who are (wrongly) of the thought that, when you cook any type of liquor, the alcohol burns off. Various studies have proved this to be wrong. Most of the alcohol will indeed be burned (evaporated) off, but if you are preparing this for anyone with an alcohol-related illness, they may have a reaction.

Ingredients

4 bananas, peeled
1 tsp. lemon juice
½ cup butter
¾ cup brown sugar
1 tsp. ground cinnamon
½ tsp. ground nutmeg
½ cup Kahlúa
¼ cup spiced rum
whipped cream, for topping

Steps

1. Cut the bananas in half lengthwise and then cut each piece in half. Sprinkle the bananas with the lemon juice (to keep them from browning) and set them aside.

2. In a medium sauté pan, melt the butter over medium heat. Stir in the brown sugar, cinnamon, and nutmeg.

3. Remove the pan from the heat and stir in the Kahlúa and rum.

4. Place the pan back onto the heat and bring the sauce to a simmer.

5. Place the bananas onto a serving platter.

6. Spoon the sauce over the bananas.

7. Dollop the bananas with some whipped cream and serve.

Southwest Candied Bacon

(Makes 1 pound)

Bacon! It's everywhere! At Casa de Cuisine, it is even in our ice cream (and you can get that recipe on page 216). Why is there such an intense love affair with bacon? It is all about flavor. The taste buds on our tongues center on two basic flavors: savory and sweet. Bacon, in many cases, features both of these flavors. Another reason for the popularity of bacon is that, for many people, it is a comfort food. If you are over the age of forty, you remember when bacon was a cheap food. There was always bacon in the house, and when it came to breakfast, it was lying there on the plate right next to some eggs and, if you really wanted to pig-out (pardon the pun), some sausage. Nowadays, bacon is getting rather expensive (thanks to supply and demand), and there are even chic flavors of the fatty stomach of porky.

If you venture into some rather ritzy eateries, you will find some dishes, both savory and sweet, which feature something called "candied bacon." What is this stuff? Simply put, it is bacon which is caramelized with sugar. A pretty simple process that you pay a lot of money for because it is . . . chic! Here in the Southwest, we take this candied bacon and give it a little pizzazz. We add chili powder—and if we really want to turn up the heat, we add a chipotle chili powder.

To make Southwest Candied Bacon is quite simple. It can also be quite messy, and it does take a few steps. The good news is that it only takes three ingredients and is not too time-consuming. You do want to use a good quality bacon, so stay away from those chemically induced bacons you find in packages at your local supermarket. Buy the bacon in the butcher section, which is simply smoked pork belly without any "juice." You can use any flavor of smoked bacon, but in this case, I would stay away from the peppered bacon as it will interfere with the sweetness.

Ingredients
1 pound sliced smoked bacon
½ cup brown sugar
1 Tbs. chili powder

Steps
1. Pre-heat your oven to 350°F. Line a baking sheet with parchment paper. Do not use a silicone baking sheet.
2. Place the bacon slices on a flat surface (such as your kitchen counter).
3. In a small bowl, combine the brown sugar and chili powder.

4. Sprinkle both sides of the bacon with the brown sugar mixture and let sit 5 minutes.

5. Place the bacon onto the prepared baking sheet in a single layer.

6. Place a sheet of foil over the bacon and then place another baking sheet on top (this will act as a weight).

7. Place into the oven and cook 30 minutes.

8. Remove the bacon from the oven. Remove the top baking sheet.

9. Carefully remove the foil from atop the bacon.

10. Remove the bacon and place on a slightly oiled plate. (The plate must be oiled because you've you just "candied" the bacon—essentially creating a caramel coating with the melted brown sugar—and you'll need to be able to easily remove it from the plate once it has cooled.)

11. Once the bacon has cooled (become candied), cut or break into serving pieces.

> ···Note···
> The thickness of the bacon will determine its texture. It is wonderful whether it is brittle or sort of chewy.

Sweet and Spicy Southwest Glazed Almonds

(Makes 2 cups)

You ever go to a bar or cantina and see salty snacks there for you to nibble on for free while you enjoy the adult beverage of your choice? There is a reason for this. The salt will dehydrate you, thus making you thirsty, and when you're thirsty, you will order another beverage. Also, they're not really "free"; the price of those snacks is built into the price of your beverage whether you eat them or not, so . . . grab a handful and enjoy! Why do I bring this up in a section on desserts? Because, most of the time, these snacks are nuts of one kind or another, and nuts also make for a great sweet and savory dessert here in the American Southwest.

If you were to study the history of desserts throughout time, you would find that the original desserts featured only fruits and nuts. Desserts, from an historical point, were meant to cleanse your palate after a meal. Both fruits and nuts have this ability. Of course, it is also quite nice that both are rather healthy, inexpensive, and readily available at any market. Sweet and Spicy Southwest Glazed Almonds are one dessert that I feature every summer when I am having an outdoor party at home. No need for dessert plates; just put a few bowls on the table and let your friends and family munch at will. A very simple dessert which will appease the taste buds of everyone!

Almonds are one of our favorite nuts here in the Southwest since we grow them by the bushel, but if you are not a fan of them, you can use whatever your favorite nut is. If you opt to use a soft variety of nut, such as a walnut or pecan, be advised that, due to the more porous texture of these nuts, the flavors of the glaze can be a little more intense—and for a dessert, some people might find this a little too much.

Ingredients

¼ cup pure maple syrup
1 tsp. garlic salt
1 tsp. chili powder
1 tsp. ground cumin
½ tsp. celery seeds
2 cups whole almonds

Steps

1. Pre-heat your oven to 350°F.

2. In a medium bowl, whisk the maple syrup, garlic salt, chili powder, cumin, and celery seeds.

3. Add the almonds and stir to coat.

4. Spoon the almonds into a large, oven-safe non-stick sauté pan or skillet.

5. Place into the oven and cook 20 minutes, stirring them about every 5 minutes.

6. Brush a baking sheet with vegetable oil.

7. Take the almonds out of the oven and place them onto the prepared baking sheet, separating them so they are individual (not sticking together).

8. Let the almonds cool.

9. If not serving right away, keep the almonds in an airtight container.

Tequila Blackberry Cobbler with Buttermilk Crust

(Makes 4 servings)

If you ever want to start a heated discussion among "foodies," bring up the dessert known as cobbler and watch the sparks fly. Why does this dessert create chaos? The name! What I refer to as a "cobbler," you may call a "crisp" or maybe a "pandowdy." You may even call it "betty" or a "crumble." It all depends on where you are from, but the dish is essentially the same. The one thing all will agree on is that, when it is served, you will want seconds.

There is another discussion which will ensue, and that has to do with the topping. Should it have a pie crust–like topping? Should it have no topping? Maybe a crumb topping? Once again, it depends on where you are from. In the case of this Tequila Blackberry Cobbler, we are going to have a buttermilk topping simply because, when you're from the Southwest, you do like to break rules in the kitchen.

We are going to be using tequila in this dessert. Why? Because we can! Also because the combination of tequila and blackberries is simply heavenly. Tequila is a liquor derived from the agave plant, and the flavor accentuates the natural sweetness of the blackberries. It is a win-win situation and delicious.

For Crust
2 cups flour
2 Tbs. sugar
1 Tbs. baking soda
½ tsp. salt
⅓ cup shortening
1 cup buttermilk

For Blackberry Filling
¼ cup butter, melted
¾ cup brown sugar
¾ cup sugar
½ cup heavy cream
¼ cup tequila
½ tsp. ground cinnamon
1 pound blackberries

Steps

1. In a medium bowl, whisk the flour, sugar, baking soda, and salt. Stir in the shortening and buttermilk to form a sticky dough. Place a piece of plastic wrap over the bowl and set aside.

2. Pre-heat your oven to 350°F.

3. In an oven-safe medium sauté pan or round au gratin pan, over medium heat, melt the butter.

4. Stir in the brown sugar, sugar, heavy cream, tequila, and cinnamon and cook until both sugars have dissolved.

5. Add the blackberries and gently toss to coat.

6. Remove the pan from the heat and dot the top with the crust mixture. Don't worry if it doesn't cover the entire cobbler; it will expand as it bakes.

7. Place into the oven and bake 25 minutes.

8. Remove from the oven and let cool before serving.

Tequila Sunrise Sorbet

(Makes about 3 cups)

One of the most popular drinks to emerge from the Southwest is also the basis for one of the most popular frozen desserts from Casa de Cuisine. A refreshing frozen dessert which will invigorate the body and soul after a sweltering day in the Southwest sun. If you enjoy a freshly made Tequila Sunrise cocktail (psst, check out page 305), you will love our Tequila Sunrise Sorbet!

Making this sorbet is a little different than other sorbets because we are going to be dealing with a liquor product which is usually about forty percent alcohol, meaning that, during the churning process, you will not get as solid a product as usual. The reason for this is that alcohol does not freeze. It can get slushy, but it cannot freeze. Have no fear—I do have a remedy for this!

You will note the basic ingredients for this Tequila Sunrise Sorbet are the same for its namesake cocktail. With this dessert, however, we will be adding more orange juice, and we will be adding a simple syrup. Both of these ingredients will help the sorbet to solidify and become scoopable as they will aid in freezing the molecules around the alcohol.

Ingredients

1 cup simple syrup (see note)
1½ cups orange juice
2 Tbs. grenadine
½ tsp. salt
2 Tbs. lime juice
¼ cup white tequila

> ··· Note ···
>
> To make your own simple syrup: Combine equal parts sugar and water in a pot, heat over medium heat, and stir until the sugar dissolves and the water is clear. That's it! Keep the simple syrup in a bottle and either refrigerate it or, if you're going to be using it often, put it in your pantry.

Steps

1. In a medium bowl, whisk the simple syrup, orange juice, grenadine, salt, and lime juice.

2. Place into the refrigerator and chill at least 2 hours.

3. Pour the mixture into an ice cream machine and follow the manufacturer's instructions.

4. Once the mixture becomes "slushy," add the tequila in a slow and steady stream while the machine is churning.

5. Freeze the Tequila Sunrise Sorbet until ready to serve. Since this has alcohol in it, you will need to freeze it after it leaves the ice cream machine to get a scoopable texture.

The Southwest Cantina

Atacama Pisco Sour

Ingredients

crushed ice
1½ ounces pisco
½ ounce Scotch
1 ounce lemon juice
1 ounce simple syrup
grated lemon zest

Steps

1. Into a blender, combine all the ingredients, except the lemon zest, and puree until smooth.

2. Pour into a margarita glass.

3. Sprinkle with some lemon zest and serve.

Batida

Ingredients

crushed ice
2 ounces cachaça
½ ounce simple syrup
½ ounce lemon juice
3 ounces pineapple juice

Steps

1. Fill a high ball glass with crushed ice.
2. Pour in each of the ingredients.
3. Stir with a swizzle stick and serve.

Batida Maracuja

Ingredients

ice cubes
2 ounces cachaça
2 passion fruit, peeled, seeded, and pureed
1 ounce simple syrup
1 ounce lemon juice
crushed ice
1 slice lemon

Steps

1. Place the ice cubes into a cocktail shaker.
2. Add the cachaça, passion fruit puree, simple syrup, and lemon juice and shake well.
3. Fill a highball glass with crushed ice.
4. Strain the Batida Maracuja into the glass.
5. Top with a slice of lemon and serve.

Caipirinha

Ingredients

½ lime, cut in half
2 tsp. sugar
crushed ice
2 ounces cachaça

Steps

1. Place the lime pieces and sugar into an old-fashioned glass. Using a spoon, press the lime against the glass (this is called muddling).

2. Fill the glass with crushed ice.

3. Pour the cachaça over the ice.

4. Stir and serve.

Cowgirl

Ingredients

1 ounce peach schnapps

½ ounce Irish cream

1 small peach wedge

Steps

1. Pour the peach schnapps into a 2-ounce shot glass.

2. Float the Irish cream on top.

3. Put a small peach wedge onto the rim of the glass and serve.

Go West

Ingredients

ice cubes
½ ounce Frangelico
1 ounce limoncello
1 ounce dry white wine
½ ounce simple syrup
½ ounce lemon juice
1 strip lemon zest

Steps

1. Place the ice into a cocktail shaker.
2. Add the remaining ingredients, except the lemon zest, and shake well.
3. Strain into a martini glass.
4. Place the zest into the drink and serve.

Grasshopper

Ingredients

1 ounce crème de cacao

1 ounce crème de menthe

½ ounce heavy cream

1 sprig of mint

Steps

1. Pour the crème de cacao into a cocktail glass.

2. Float the crème de menthe over the crème de cacao.

3. Float the heavy cream on top.

4. Add the sprig of mint and serve.

Original Pisco Sour

Ingredients

ice cubes
2 ounces pisco
1 ounce lemon juice
2 tsp. sugar
1 egg white
3 dashes Angostura aromatic bitters
1 lemon wedge

Steps

1. Place the ice cubes into a cocktail shaker.
2. Add the pisco, lemon juice, sugar, and egg white and shake well.
3. Strain into an old-fashioned glass.
4. Add the bitters to the frothy head (created by the egg white).
5. Place a lemon wedge on the rim of the glass and serve.

Q.F.

Ingredients

½ ounce Kahlúa
¼ ounce Midori
½ ounce Irish cream

Steps

1. Pour the Kahlúa into a 2-ounce shot glass.
2. Float the Midori over the Kahlúa.
3. Float the Irish cream over the Midori

> ··· Note ···
>
> As for the name of this drink. The initial "Q" stands for "quick," and the initial "F" stands for a word never used in a cookbook!

Velvet Hammer

Ingredients

ice cubes
1 ounce Cointreau
1 ounce Tia Maria
1 ounce heavy cream

Steps

1. Place the ice cubes into a cocktail shaker.

2. Add the Cointreau, Tia Maria, and heavy cream and shake well.

3. Strain into a cocktail glass and serve.

Black Widow

Ingredients

ice cubes
2 ounces dark rum
1 ounce Southern Comfort
1 ounce lime juice
½ ounce simple syrup
1 slice lime

Steps

1. Place the ice into a cocktail shaker.
2. Add the dark rum, Southern Comfort, lime juice, and simple syrup and shake well.
3. Strain into a cocktail glass.
4. Place a slice of lime on the rim of the glass and serve.

Bolero

Ingredients
ice cubes
1½ ounces light rum
¾ ounce apple brandy
½ ounce sweet vermouth
lemon zest

Steps
1. Put some ice into a cocktail shaker.
2. Add the rum, apple brandy, and sweet vermouth and shake well.
3. Strain into a cocktail glass and add 2 ice cubes.
4. Add the lemon zest and serve.

Cooper Cooler

Ingredients

ice cubes
2 ounces gold rum
3 ounces ginger ale
1 Tbs. lime juice
1 slice lime

Steps

1. Put the ice into a highball glass.
2. Pour the gold rum, ginger ale, and lime juice over the ice.
3. Place the slice of lime on the rim of the glass and serve.

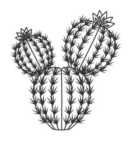

Cuba Libra

Ingredients
ice cubes
1 ounce gold rum
1 ounce lime juice
cola
1 lime wedge

Steps
1. Fill a highball glass with ice.
2. Pour in the rum and lime juice and stir.
3. Top with the cola.
4. Place the lime wedge on the rim of the glass and serve.

El Dorado

Ingredients

ice cubes
1 ounce light rum
1 ounce advocaat
1 ounce crème de cacao
2 tsp. grated coconut

Steps

1. Place the ice cubes into a cocktail shaker.
2. Add the rum, advocaat, crème de cacao, and coconut and shake well.
3. Strain into a chilled cocktail glass and serve.

Frozen Mango and Mint Spiced Daiquiri

Ingredients

crushed ice
1 ounce lime juice
2 tsp. simple syrup
2 ounces spiced rum
½ mango, chopped
6 mint leaves
1 mint leaf with the stem

Steps

1. Into a blender, add the ice, lime juice, simple syrup, spiced rum, mango, and 6 mint leaves and puree.

2. Pour into a chilled champagne glass.

3. Top with a sprig of mint and serve.

Frozen Mango Daiquiri

Ingredients

crushed ice
½ mango, chopped
1 ounce lime juice
2 ounces light rum
1 tsp. powdered sugar

Steps

1. Place all of the ingredients into a blender.

2. Puree until smooth.

3. Pour into a large chilled cocktail glass and serve.

Gauguin

Ingredients

crushed ice
2 ounces light rum
2 tsp. passion fruit syrup
2 tsp. lemon juice
1 tsp. lime juice
1 maraschino cherry

Steps

1. Place everything, except the cherry, into a blender and puree.
2. Strain the drink into a cocktail glass.
3. Top with a cherry and serve.

Grenada

Ingredients

ice cubes
½ orange, juice only
1 ounce sweet vermouth
3 ounces dark rum
1 cinnamon stick

Steps

1. Place the ice into a cocktail shaker.
2. Add the orange juice, sweet vermouth, and rum and shake well.
3. Strain into a chilled cocktail glass.
4. Stir with a cinnamon stick and serve.

Hummingbird

Ingredients

ice cubes
1 ounce dark rum
1 ounce light rum
1 ounce Southern Comfort
1 ounce orange juice
cola
1 orange slice

Steps

1. Place the ice cubes into a cocktail shaker.
2. Add both rums, Southern Comfort, and orange juice and shake well.
3. Strain into a chilled tall glass.
4. Top with the cola.
5. Place an orange slice on the rim of the glass and serve.

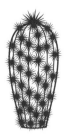

Limon Mojito

Ingredients

1 lime, quartered
2 tsp. brown sugar
8 mint leaves
crushed ice
2 ounces limon rum
1 slice lemon
1 slice lime

Steps

1. In a cocktail shaker, place the quarters of lime, brown sugar, and mint. With a spoon (or muddler), crush them all together.

2. Fill a highball glass with crushed ice. Set aside.

3. Add the rum to the cocktail shaker and shake well.

4. Strain into the glass with crushed ice.

5. Place a lemon and lime slice on the rim of the glass and serve.

Mojito

Ingredients

8 mint leaves
½ lime, cut into wedges
2 tsp. sugar
crushed ice
2½ ounces light rum
soda water
2 mint sprigs

Steps

1. Place the mint, lime, and sugar into a cocktail shaker. With a spoon, crush them together (or use a muddler).

2. Fill a highball glass with crushed ice. Set aside.

3. Pour the rum into the cocktail shaker and shake well.

4. Strain the rum mixture into the glass with crushed ice.

5. Top with some soda water.

6. Add 2 mint sprigs and serve.

The Papa Doble

Ingredients

crushed ice
3 ounces light rum
½ ounce maraschino liqueur
1 ounce lime juice
1½ ounces grapefruit juice
1 small grapefruit wedge

Steps

1. Into a blender, add some crushed ice, rum, maraschino liqueur, lime juice, and grapefruit juice and puree.

2. Pour the mixture into a tall chilled glass.

3. Place a small grapefruit wedge on the rim of the glass and serve.

Piña Colada

Ingredients

crushed ice
1 ounce light rum
2 ounces coconut milk
2 ounces pineapple juice
1 small pineapple wedge

Steps

1. Place the crushed ice, rum, coconut milk, and pineapple juice into a cocktail shaker and shake well.

2. Strain the mixture into a chilled class.

3. Place a pineapple wedge on the rim of the glass and serve.

Pineapple Mojito

Ingredients
6 mint leaves
4 pieces of pineapple
2 tsp. brown sugar
2 ounces dark rum
crushed ice
pineapple juice
1 sprig mint

Steps
1. Into a cocktail shaker, add the mint leaves, pineapple pieces, and brown sugar. With a spoon, crush them all together (or use a muddler).
2. Add the rum and shake well.
3. Place crushed ice in a highball glass. Strain the rum mixture into the glass.
4. Top with the pineapple juice.
5. Place a sprig of mint in the glass and serve.

Pink Mojito

Ingredients

6 mint leaves
½ lime, cut into quarters
2 tsp. simple syrup
3 raspberries
crushed ice
1½ ounces light rum
½ ounce Chambord
cranberry juice
1 sprig mint

Steps

1. Into a cocktail shaker, place the mint leaves, lime, simple syrup, and raspberries. Crush them together with a spoon (or use a muddler).

2. Place the crushed ice into a chilled highball glass. Set aside.

3. Into the cocktail strainer, add the light rum and Chambord and shake well.

4. Strain over the crushed ice and stir.

5. Top with the cranberry juice.

6. Add a sprig of mint and serve.

Port Antonio

Ingredients

½ tsp. grenadine
ice cubes
1 ounce lime juice
3 ounces gold rum
1 strip lime zest
1 maraschino cherry

Steps

1. Add the grenadine to a cocktail glass. Set aside.
2. Into a cocktail shaker, add the ice, lime juice, and rum and shake well.
3. Strain into the cocktail glass with grenadine.
4. Into the drink, place the lime zest and cherry and serve.

Rum Crusta

Ingredients

1 tsp. sugar
1 lime wedge
2 ounces dark rum
1 ounce Cointreau
2 tsp. grenadine
2 tsp. lime juice
crushed ice

Steps

1. Place sugar on a small plate and set aside. Rub the rim of an old-fashioned glass with the lime wedge, then press glass into the sugar, so the sugar adheres to the rim.

2. Fill the old-fashioned glass with crushed ice (be careful not to brush the sugar off the rim).

3. Into a cocktail shaker, add the rum, Cointreau, grenadine, and lime juice and shake well.

4. Pour the mixture over the crushed ice and serve.

Rum Old-Fashioned

Ingredients

ice cubes
1 dash Angostura aromatic bitters
½ ounce lime juice
1 tsp. sugar
½ ounce water
2 ounces light rum
½ ounce dark rum

Steps

1. Place 1 ice cube into a chilled old-fashioned glass and then stir in the bitters, lime juice, sugar, and water until the sugar has dissolved.

2. Add both rums and more ice and serve.

Serenade

Ingredients
ice cubes
1 ounce light rum
½ ounce Disaronno amaretto
½ ounce coconut cream
2 ounces pineapple juice

Steps
1. Into a blender, add 3 ice cubes, rum, Disaronno amaretto, coconut cream, and pineapple juice and puree.
2. Place some ice cubes into a chilled tall glass.
3. Pour the mixture into the glass and serve.

Tobago

Ingredients
½ ounce light rum
½ ounce gin
1 tsp. lime juice
1 tsp. guava syrup
crushed ice

Steps
1. Into a cocktail shaker, add the rum, gin, lime juice, and guava syrup and shake well.
2. Fill a cocktail glass with crushed ice.
3. Pour the mixture over the ice and serve.

Yellow Bird

Ingredients

ice cubes
1½ ounces light rum
1 ounce lime juice
½ ounce Galliano
½ ounce triple sec

Steps

1. Into a cocktail shaker, add some ice, rum, lime juice, Galliano, and triple sec and shake well.

2. Strain the mixture into a chilled cocktail glass and serve.

Acapulco Bliss

Ingredients

ice cubes

1 ounce gold tequila

1 Tbs. banana liqueur

2 tsp. Galliano

1 ounce lime juice

3⅓ ounces passion fruit juice

1 ounce heavy cream

1 slice lemon

1 sprig mint

Steps

1. Place the ice cubes into a cocktail shaker.

2. Add the remaining ingredients, except the lemon slice and mint, and shake very well.

3. Pour the mixture into a chilled sling glass.

4. Place the slice of lemon on the rim of the glass.

5. Place the sprig of mint in the drink and serve.

Agave Julep

Ingredients

8 mint leaves
1 Tbs. simple syrup
1½ ounces gold tequila
1¼ ounces lime juice
crushed ice
1 lime wedge
1 mint sprig

Steps

1. In a cocktail shaker, add the mint leaves and simple syrup; mash together with a spoon (or a muddler).

2. Add the tequila and lime juice and shake well.

3. Fill a julep glass with crushed ice.

4. Pour the mixture over the ice and stir.

5. Place a lime wedge on the rim of the glass.

6. Place a sprig of mint in the drink and serve.

Baja Sour

Ingredients

ice cubes
1¼ ounces gold tequila
2 tsp. simple syrup
1¼ ounces lemon juice
2 dashes orange bitters
½ egg white
1 Tbs. sweet sherry
1 lemon slice

Steps

1. Into a cocktail shaker, place all the ingredients, except the sherry and lemon slice, and shake well.
2. Pour into a large chilled glass.
3. Float the sherry over the drink.
4. Place a slice of lemon on the rim of the glass and serve.

Batanga

Ingredients

1 tsp. sea salt
1 lime, quartered
ice cubes
2 ounces gold tequila
cola

Steps

1. Place sea salt on a small plate and set aside. Rub the rim of a highball glass with a lime wedge, then press glass into the salt, so the salt adheres to the rim.

2. Fill the glass with ice (be careful not to brush the salt off the rim).

3. Pour the tequila over the ice.

4. Squeeze the juice from the remaining limes into the glass.

5. Top with the cola and serve.

Border Crossing

Ingredients

ice cubes
1½ ounces gold tequila
1 ounce lime juice
1 ounce honey
4 dashes orange bitters
3 ounces ginger ale
1 lime wedge

Steps

1. Fill a cocktail shaker with ice cubes.
2. Add the remaining ingredients, except the ginger ale and lime, and shake well.
3. Strain the mixture into a chilled highball glass.
4. Top with the ginger ale.
5. Place a lime wedge on the rim of the glass and serve.

Brave Bull

Ingredients

ice cubes
1 ounce white tequila
1 ounce Kahlúa

Steps

1. Fill an old-fashioned glass with ice.
2. Pour in the tequila.
3. Float the Kahlúa on top and gently stir.

Cobalt Margarita

Ingredients

1 tsp. sea salt
1 lime wedge
ice cubes
1¼ ounces white tequila
2 tsp. Cointreau
½ ounce blue curaçao
¾ ounce lime juice
¾ ounce grapefruit juice
1 strip lime zest

Steps

1. Place sea salt on a small plate and set aside. Rub the rim of a margarita glass with a lime wedge, then press glass into the salt, so the salt adheres to the rim.

2. Fill a cocktail shaker with ice.

3. Add the remaining ingredients, except the lime zest, and shake well.

4. Strain the mixture into a margarita glass (be careful not to brush the salt off the rim).

5. Place the lime zest atop the drink and serve.

Desert Daisy

Ingredients

crushed ice
1 ounce white tequila
1¼ ounces lime juice
2 tsp. simple syrup
1 Tbs. crème de fraise de bois
1 lime wedge
1 mint sprig

Steps

1. Fill an old-fashioned glass halfway with ice.

2. Add the tequila, lime juice, and simple syrup and gently stir.

3. Add more ice.

4. Top with the crème de fraise de bois.

5. Place a lime wedge on the rim of the glass and a sprig of mint in the drink and serve.

Dirty Sanchez

Ingredients

ice cubes
2 tsp. dry vermouth
2 ounces gold tequila
2 tsp. olive brine (from a can of black olives)
2 black olives, pitted

Steps

1. Fill a cocktail shaker with ice.
2. Add the vermouth, tequila, and olive brine and shake well.
3. Strain the mixture into a chilled cocktail glass.
4. Add the olives and serve.

El Diablo

Ingredients

ice cubes
1¼ ounces gold tequila
¾ ounce lime juice
2 tsp. grenadine
3½ ounces ginger ale
1 slice lime

Steps

1. Fill a highball glass with ice.
2. Add the tequila, lime juice, and grenadine and lightly stir.
3. Top with the ginger ale.
4. Add a slice of lime and serve.

Grand Margarita

Ingredients

1 tsp. sea salt
1 lime wedge
ice cubes
1½ ounces white tequila
1 ounce Grand Marnier
1 ounce lime juice

Steps

1. Place sea salt on a small plate and set aside. Rub the rim of a chilled margarita glass with a lime wedge, then press glass into the salt, so the salt adheres to the rim.

2. Place ice cubes into a cocktail shaker.

3. Add the tequila, Grand Marnier, and lime juice and shake well.

4. Strain the mixture into the margarita glass and serve (be careful not to brush the salt from the rim of the glass).

Jalisco Swizzle

Ingredients

ice cubes
3 dashes Angostura aromatic bitters
¾ ounce gold tequila
¾ ounce gold rum
1¼ ounces lime juice
¾ ounce passion fruit juice
2 tsp. simple syrup
crushed ice
1 ounce soda water
1 slice lime

Steps

1. Put the ice cubes into a cocktail shaker.
2. Add the bitters, tequila, rum, lime juice, passion fruit juice, and simple syrup and shake well.
3. Fill a highball glass with crushed ice.
4. Strain the mixture into the glass.
5. Top with the soda water.
6. Place a slice of lime on the rim of the glass and serve.

Maracuja

Ingredients

1 passion fruit, peeled, seeded, and fruit pureed
ice cubes
1¼ ounces gold tequila
1 Tbs. Cointreau
¾ ounce lime juice
1 tsp. passion fruit syrup

Steps

1. Into a cocktail shaker, place the pureed passion fruit, ice, tequila, Cointreau, lime juice, and passion fruit syrup and shake well.

2. Strain into a chilled cocktail glass and serve.

Margarita

Ingredients

1 tsp. sea salt
1 lime wedge
ice cubes
2 ounces gold tequila
1 ounce lime juice
1 ounce triple sec
1 slice lime

Steps

1. Place sea salt on a small plate and set aside. Rub the rim of a chilled margarita glass with a lime wedge, then press glass into the salt, so the salt adheres to the rim.

2. Place some ice cubes into a cocktail shaker.

3. Add the tequila, lime juice, and triple sec and shake well.

4. Strain into a margarita glass (be careful not to brush the salt from the rim of the glass).

5. Place a slice of lime onto the rim of the glass and serve.

Mexican Bulldog

Ingredients

ice cubes
¾ ounce gold tequila
¼ ounce Kahlúa
1¼ ounces heavy cream
3½ ounces cola
dash of cocoa powder

Steps

1. Place the ice cubes into a cocktail shaker.
2. Add the tequila, Kahlúa, and cream and shake well.
3. Strain the mixture into a highball glass.
4. Top with the cola and gently stir.
5. Sprinkle with the cocoa powder and serve.

Mexican Mule

Ingredients

1 lime, sliced
1 tsp. simple syrup
crushed ice
1 ounce gold tequila
1 ounce Kahlúa
ginger ale to top

Steps

1. Place the lime and simple syrup into a highball glass; using a spoon, mash them together (or use a muddler).

2. Fill the glass halfway with crushed ice.

3. Add the tequila and Kahlúa.

4. Top with the ginger ale and serve.

Mexicana

Ingredients

ice cubes
1¼ ounces white tequila
¾ ounce framboise
¾ ounce lemon juice
3½ ounces pineapple juice
1 lemon slice

Steps

1. Place some ice into a cocktail shaker.
2. Add the tequila, framboise, lemon juice, and pineapple juice and shake well.
3. Place some ice cubes into a highball glass.
4. Strain the mixture into the glass.
5. Add the lemon slice into the drink and serve.

Mexicola

Ingredients

1 lime, cut into 4 wedges
crushed ice
1½ ounces tequila
6 ounces cola

Steps

1. Place the lime wedges into a tall highball glass and mash them with a spoon (or use a muddler).

2. Fill the glass with crushed ice.

3. Add the tequila and cola, gently stir, and serve.

Pancho Villa

Ingredients
ice cubes
1 ounce gold tequila
½ ounce Tia Maria
1 tsp. Cointreau

Steps
1. Place some ice cubes into a cocktail shaker.
2. Add the tequila, Tia Maria, and Cointreau and shake well.
3. Strain into a chilled cocktail glass and serve.

Playa Del Mar

Ingredients

1 tsp. sea salt
1 Tbs. brown sugar
1 orange slice
ice cubes
1¼ ounces gold tequila
¾ ounce Grand Marnier
2 tsp. lime juice
¾ ounce cranberry juice
¾ ounce pineapple juice
1 strip orange zest

Steps

1. In a small bowl, blend the salt and brown sugar; set aside. Rub the orange slice around the rim of a chilled sling glass, then press the glass into the salt–brown sugar mixture so it adheres to the rim.
2. Fill the sling glass with ice (be careful not to brush the salt–brown sugar mixture off the rim).
3. Into a cocktail shaker, add the tequila, Grand Marnier, lime juice, cranberry juice, and pineapple juice and shake well.
4. Strain the mixture into the sling glass.
5. Add the orange zest to the top of the drink and serve.

Rosarita Bay Breeze

Ingredients

ice cubes
1¼ ounces white tequila
6 ounces cranberry juice
1½ ounces pineapple juice
1 orange slice

Steps

1. Place the ice cubes into a highball glass.
2. Pour in the tequila and cranberry juice.
3. Float the pineapple juice atop.
4. Place the orange slice on the rim of the glass and serve.

Ruby Rita

Ingredients

1 tsp. sea salt
1¼ ounces pink grapefruit juice
ice cubes
1¼ ounces gold tequila
¾ ounce Cointreau

Steps

1. Place sea salt on a small plate and set aside. Rub the rim of a highball glass with some of the pink grapefruit juice, then press glass into the salt, so the salt adheres to the rim.

2. Fill the glass with ice (be careful not to brush the salt off the rim).

3. Pour into the glass the remaining grapefruit juice, tequila, and Cointreau.

4. Slightly stir the drink and serve.

Sombrero

Ingredients

ice cubes

¾ ounce tequila

¾ ounce white crème de cacao

3½ ounces heavy cream

dash of grated nutmeg

Steps

1. Place the ice into a cocktail shaker.

2. Add the tequila, white crème de cacao, and heavy cream and shake well.

3. Strain into a chilled margarita glass.

4. Sprinkle with nutmeg and serve.

South for the Summer

Ingredients

2 tsp. grenadine
crushed ice
2 ounces white tequila
3 ounces orange juice
4 pieces (cubes) pineapple
1 strip orange zest

Steps

1. Pour the grenadine into a highball glass.

2. Into a blender, place the crushed ice, tequila, orange juice, and pineapple and puree.

3. Pour into the highball glass.

4. Place the orange zest atop the drink and serve.

South of the Border

Ingredients
ice cubes
1¼ ounces gold tequila
¾ ounce Kahlúa
1¼ ounces lime juice

Steps
1. Place some ice cubes into a cocktail shaker.
2. Add the tequila, Kahlúa, and lime juice and shake well.
3. Strain into a chilled cocktail glass and serve.

Sunburn

Ingredients

ice cubes
¾ ounce gold tequila
1 Tbs. Cointreau
6 ounces cranberry juice
1 orange slice

Steps

1. Fill a highball glass with ice.
2. Add the tequila, Cointreau, and cranberry juice.
3. Place the orange slice on the rim of the glass and serve.

Tijuana Sling

Ingredients
ice cubes
1¼ ounces white tequila
¾ ounce crème de cassis
¾ ounce lime juice
2 dashes Angostura aromatic bitters
3½ ounces ginger ale
1 slice lime

Steps
1. Place the ice into a cocktail shaker.
2. Add the tequila, crème de cassis, lime juice, and bitters and shake well.
3. Strain into a chilled highball glass.
4. Top with the ginger ale.
5. Place the slice of lime on the rim of the glass and serve.

Tequila de Coco

Ingredients

crushed ice
1 ounce white tequila
1 ounce lemon juice
1 ounce coconut syrup
3¼ ounces grenadine
1 slice lemon

Steps

1. Into a blender, add some crushed ice, tequila, lemon juice, coconut syrup, and grenadine and puree.

2. Pour the mixture into a chilled tall glass.

3. Place the lemon slice on the rim of the glass and serve.

Tequila Slammer

Ingredients

1 ounce gold tequila

1 ounce champagne

Steps

1. Pour the tequila into a 2-ounce shot glass.

2. Slowly top the tequila with the champagne.

3. Hold the glass tightly with your palm firmly covering the top.

4. Slam the glass down on a surface to create a fizz and then drink it in one gulp.

Tequila Sunrise

Ingredients

ice cubes
2 ounces gold tequila
4 ounces orange juice
2 tsp. grenadine
1 orange slice

Steps

1. Place some ice into a cocktail shaker.
2. Add the tequila and orange juice and shake well.
3. Fill a chilled tall glass with ice.
4. Strain the mixture into the glass.
5. Top the drink with the grenadine.
6. Place an orange slice onto the rim of the glass and serve.

Tequini

Ingredients

ice cubes
3 dashes orange bitters
3 ounces white tequila
2 tsp. dry vermouth
1 black olive

Steps

1. Place the ice into a cocktail shaker.

2. Add the orange bitters, tequila, and dry vermouth and shake well.

3. Strain the mixture into a chilled martini glass.

4. Add the black olive and serve.

Texas Tea

Ingredients

ice cubes
¾ ounce gold tequila
1 Tbs. white rum
2 tsp. simple syrup
¾ ounce lemon juice
¾ ounce orange juice
3½ ounces black tea
1 sprig of mint

Steps

1. Place some ice into a cocktail shaker.
2. Add the tequila, white rum, simple syrup, lemon juice, orange juice, and tea and shake well.
3. Strain the mixture into a chilled sling glass.
4. Place a sprig of mint into the drink and serve.

Viva Maria

Ingredients
ice cubes
1 ounce tequila
½ ounce lime juice
¼ ounce grenadine
½ egg white
crushed ice
1 maraschino cherry

Steps

1. Place some ice cubes into a cocktail shaker.
2. Add the tequila, lime juice, grenadine, and egg white and shake well.
3. Fill a champagne glass with crushed ice.
4. Strain the mixture into the glass.
5. Top with a cherry and serve.

Casa Sangria

Ingredients

2 bottles chilled dry red wine
½ cup spiced rum
½ cup orange juice
¼ cup sugar
2 oranges, peeled and thinly sliced
2 lemons, peeled and thinly sliced
2 limes, peeled and thinly sliced
club soda

Steps

1. In a large bowl or pitcher, stir the wine, rum, orange juice, and sugar until very well blended.

2. Add the oranges, lemons, and limes.

3. Chill at least 2 hours.

4. Top each serving with some club soda.

Rosé Sangria

Ingredients

1 bottle rosé wine
¼ cup sugar
½ pint raspberries
1 cup sliced strawberries
1 lime, thinly sliced
1 orange, thinly sliced
club soda

Steps

1. In a pitcher, stir the rosé wine and sugar until the sugar has dissolved.

2. Add the raspberries, strawberries, lime, and orange and give a few stirs.

3. Chill at least 2 hours before serving.

4. Top each serving with some club soda.

Summer Sangria

Ingredients

1 bottle dry white wine
¼ cup sugar
1 lime, thinly sliced
1 lemon, thinly sliced
1 peach, peeled and cut into 8 wedges
1 mango, peeled and cubed
½ pint raspberries
8 slightly crushed fresh mint leaves
club soda

Steps

1. In a pitcher, stir the wine and sugar until the sugar has dissolved.

2. Add the lime, lemon, peach, mango, and raspberries and give a few stirs.

3. Chill the Summer Sangria at least 2 hours before serving.

4. Just before serving, stir in the mint leaves.

5. Top each serving with some club soda.

Index

Conversion Charts

METRIC AND IMPERIAL CONVERSIONS
(These conversions are rounded for convenience)

Ingredient	Cups/Tablespoons/Teaspoons	Ounces	Grams/Milliliters
Butter	1 cup = 16 tablespoons = 2 sticks	8 ounces	230 grams
Cheese, shredded	1 cup	4 ounces	110 grams
Cream cheese	1 tablespoon	0.5 ounce	14.5 grams
Cornstarch	1 tablespoon	0.3 ounce	8 grams
Flour, all-purpose	1 cup/1 tablespoon	4.5 ounces/0.3 ounce	125 grams/8 grams
Flour, whole wheat	1 cup	4 ounces	120 grams
Fruit, dried	1 cup	4 ounces	120 grams
Fruits or veggies, chopped	1 cup	5 to 7 ounces	145 to 200 grams
Fruits or veggies, puréed	1 cup	8.5 ounces	245 grams
Honey, maple syrup, or corn syrup	1 tablespoon	.75 ounce	20 grams
Liquids: cream, milk, water, or juice	1 cup	8 fluid ounces	240 milliliters
Oats	1 cup	5.5 ounces	150 grams
Salt	1 teaspoon	0.2 ounce	6 grams
Spices: cinnamon, cloves, ginger, or nutmeg (ground)	1 teaspoon	0.2 ounce	5 milliliters
Sugar, brown, firmly packed	1 cup	7 ounces	200 grams
Sugar, white	1 cup/1 tablespoon	7 ounces/0.5 ounce	200 grams/12.5 grams
Vanilla extract	1 teaspoon	0.2 ounce	4 grams

OVEN TEMPERATURES

Fahrenheit	Celsius	Gas Mark
225°	110°	¼
250°	120°	½
275°	140°	1
300°	150°	2
325°	160°	3
350°	180°	4
375°	190°	5
400°	200°	6
425°	220°	7
450°	230°	8